The Wines of Italy

Luigi Veronelli

The Wines of Italy

McGraw-Hill Book Company

New York

[1965]

*TP559
.I8 V4
copy 2*

Library of Congress Catalog Card Number: 64-19614

67408

Printed in Italy by Canesi Editore S.r.l., Rome

Index

Introduction

Italy is a natural wine-producing country on account of its climate, its very old traditions and its soil.

Vine growing has been, for centuries, the cultivation which has provided most of the labour of our people; this is still true to day, oddly enough when one realises that nearly one quarter of the entire population, about twelve million people, is active in the vine and wine industry.

One may therefore rightly wonder that so little attention has been paid, until a few years ago, to the problems of the vine, almost to the point of considering harmful the extraordinary variety of wines which are obtained in this ancient land of Enotria, which runs from the high Alpine valleys down to the extreme point of Sicily (and even further down to Pantelleria).

However, things are different to-day: the vine-growers have become careful, they have studied and experimented, and sometimes they have sacrificed quantity for quality and they realised at once that this extraordinary variety of wines is one of our major riches. Nowadays the password of our oenology is: "Italy

13

is not only a great producer of wines, but above all a producer of great wines".

The aim of this book is to offer the readers a careful and objective description if not of all Italian wines at least of those which, through fame and the constancy of their quality, have become established. It will be like leading the indulgent and curious reader on a fast and scintillating walk through the Italian provinces. As a matter of fact, it is surprising to realise how the wine reproduces, region by region, the beauty, the virtues and the defects of the country where it is made.

As we have said, the vine spreads out its roots from the eternal glaciers to the orange groves of Sicily and, by some strange magic, feeds itself and absorbs and retains in its products, first in the grapes and then in the wine, the essence of ancient and modern customs, which are known but unexpected, of enthusiatic and hospitable populations.

To know the wines through these pages and then, certainly with increasing pleasure, to taste them will therefore be like enjoying the thousands and thousands of panoramas of this our Italy, the garden of the world, a country now and forever pre-minently agricultural, between its warm seas and its blue skies.

I shall be satisfied if, through my work, I contribute to making readers from other countries become friends of my country, to such a point that they will never more be able to forego its wines. My hope is that an army of bottles, each one bearing its own label with its beautiful name openly displayed almost like a banner, will invade the tables of the entire world.

The Wines of Italy

Baugin: La desserré de gaufrettes

It is an established fact that wine and above all great wine is partly a matter of good luck.

Wine is the result of a succession of coincidences which are neither entirely accidental nor entirely calculated. Among the factors which work together towards its birth are the following:

— the choice of one or more varieties of vine and their biological balance, furthered by a succession of meteorological conditions;

— the soil, with the presence or absence of specific rare substances, and with its reactions to rain and drought;

— the climate, with all its components, among which the amount of sunshine is of particular importance;

— finally, man, whose every act, from the cultivation of the vine to the so-called wine-making, conditions the resulting wine. It is difficult to become a vine-dresser: love for wine is passed down from generation to generation, like a bridge between the past and the present.

Four elements, therefore, contribute to the production of

the wine: the vine, the soil, the climate and man's labour. To obtain a great wine of constant organic characteristics, not only is it necessary to have all four of these elements, but also that their conditions should always remain the same.

It is this severe law of nature which, for instance, prevents Barbaresco wine from being produced outside a certain restricted area, which prescribes the most rigid examination and unceasing selection in the introduction of modern systems of cultivation and production and which recommends, for the planting of new vines, a meticulous investigation into the nature of the vine, the soil, the exposure and the methods of cultivation.

A great wine is a harmonious creation of such perfection that the alteration of but one of the conditions of these elements is sufficient to destroy its balance.

Here we will examine objectively the wines produced from Italian vines, in Italian soil, in the Italian climate and by Italian vine-dressers.

The preservation of wine

Bottling

Good wines, which are stored in barrels, become old more or less rapidly, up to the point of losing, in the course of time, most of their qualities. It is therefore advisable to bottle the wine once it has reached its optimum, having rested and clarified in barrels.

In the barrels, the action of the oxygen, not only on the alcohol but also on the colouring elements, causes a deposit; it also assists in the development of the so-called "bouquet". However, if the oxygenation is too prolonged, the bouquet completely disappears and the wine "breaks". The optimum period is, therefore, when the wine reaches that particular condition of maturation for which it is not advisable to leave it any longer in containers which sweat and which, in any case, do not guarantee hermetic sealing.

Generally this period coincides with the month of March following the grape-harvest; there are, however, wines, above all full-bodied and very alcoholic ones, which need to remain in barrels not only for several months but for years.

When bottled, the wines should be absolutely sound and perfectly limpid, that is as clear as possible in order to prevent excess sediment in the bottles.

Thus the right time for bottling, and I want to stress this point, is an extremely fleeting state of grace and varies according to the quality or the vintage year. When done too late, the wine is old (technically it is said that the wine has been "dried" because of the unpleasant bitter taste which remains after drinking); when done too early, there is the risk of re-fermentation and of deposits.

The careful vine-grower has long since ascertained that the moon has a great influence and for nothing in the world will he bottle his wine when the moon is new. He will wait for the last quarter. This, however, is not enough: the day must be dry and clear, and the wind must not blow from the sea.

The bottles must be of good glass, suitable and strong, and perfectly clean.

There is not always sufficient control of both the glass from which the bottles are made and of their shape. The glass must, in fact, be of perfect quality and the dimensions must be uniform all the way up the bottle, that is, absolutely round both in the cylindrical part and in that which narrows to form the neck.

It is always advisable to wash the bottles with hot water containing 10% of bicarbonate of soda, then rinse them in cold water, possibly scraping the insides with a special metal brush, and finally to dry them.

Once the bottles have been carefully washed inside, they should be left to drain with the greatest care until they are perfectly dry; slight humidity is, in fact, enough to make the wine become mouldy. It is advisable therefore to put the bottles upside down in an airy, dry place. At the moment of bottling, the bottles should be at the same temperature as the wine to prevent any physical "shocks".

A last recommendation: if you do your own bottling in your own cellar, do not move the barrel or the demijohn for several days beforehand, and keep it on a high level which will permit syphoning with a rubber tube. In order not to suck up sediment, this tube should not fall more than two inches from the bottom; this is obtained by tying it to a rigid rod which holds it in place. The bottling should be done in such a way that prevents the wine coming into contact with the air as much as possible.

The cork, whole, elastic and without angles, should be neither too hard nor too soft. If old corks are used, it is advisable to soak them for 24 hours in water containing 10% of sulphuric acid and then to wash them in boiling water. Before using them, they are put in tepid water and then soaked for ¼ hour in the same wine which is to be bottled. Some people rub them over with olive oil of very recent production in order to make them more air-tight, to isolate them from the wine and to facilitate their insertion into the bottles. About an inch of space is left between the cork and the wine. Once the bottling is completed, it is advisable to leave the bottles standing upright for at least 24 hours; the cork will cling very closely to the internal sides of the neck before being wetted by the wine.

The bottles are generally laid on their sides, not tilted too much, so that the top is almost imperceptibly higher than the centre of the bottom, the cork is soaked in the wine and the air-bubble remains in the middle of the bottle. It is very important for the bottom of the cork to be completely wetted by the wine (this avoids the drying up of the cork through the passing of air and consequent oxidation). This custom of keeping the bottles horizontal is useful when the corks are of good quality; if they are not, the wine could take on an unpleasant taste from them and depreciate. Particular attention must therefore be paid to their selection.

It was once believed that leaving the bottles upright and horizontal alternately, in any case an inadvisable method, provoked the so-called "cork taste". To-day it is known to be due to an actual disease of the cork, which appears in the form of a mould and which darkens the outer holes of the cork. It is sufficient to eliminate them by making small incisions on the bottom of

23

the cork itself — the part which will come into contact with the wine — before inserting it into the bottle.

Certain wines, when kept a long time in bottles, deposit sediment of varying consistency on the bottom; when the wine is poured out, this sediment easily makes it become cloudy. This inconvenience can be reduced by three or four decantings if done in time and with great care to avoid the danger of oxidation. However, this does not always avoid the forming of deposits; many wines continue, even if very slowly, to ferment, thus creating those aromatic qualities which make them great, but also creating those insoluble products which partly cling to the sides and partly collect on the bottom of the bottle.

In order to speed up maturation of wines, and to make them become dry, the Romans exposed the full amphoras to the Summer sun, on the roofs of the houses. This custom has never been interrupted in Italy; it is often found in farms where they keep demijohns and both large and small bottles in the lofts, if not directly exposed to the rays of the sun. Some oenologists still advise accelerating maturation of wine, after bottling, by putting it, for a certain time, in stoves or in rooms facing South or in the sun. This is convenient for wines of high alcohol content and for liqueur wines; it would not be so for those of low alcohol content which, when exposed to a temperature higher than 68 degrees F., easily become sour.

I hope I have made it clear that bottling is not a common imprisonment, but a delicate sojourn of the wine under the best conditions for its evolution. Not a "confinement" but rather a spiritual "retreat", in meditation. Incidentally, the wine, if bottled by you, should be left to rest first for at least ten days in a temperate place, neither hot nor cold, so that it may recover from the journey.

For all these reasons, for that miracle of balance which is wine, for the hundreds of elements of which it is composed, capable of reacting one to the other (under the influence of external factors: heat, cold, disturbances; or of chemical agents such as oxygen from the air), for the danger of bacteria and germs which swarm in the air, allow me to give one piece of advice: buy wine, even if from the simplest peasant, already bottled, even at the cost of losing that touch of poetry which is imparted by bottling in your own cellar.

Experience has taught me that the magic balance of which I have spoken is acquired only in the cellar where the wine was born and slowly matured. Everything there has been ordered with wise laziness, in a propitious atmosphere, far from every sound.

The Cellar

Never, as in these years, has there been so much construction, but neither has such an important place as the cellar been so neglected. Modern building, with the excuse of the tyrannic necessity to exploit space, tends to eliminate it altogether.

This is neither right nor intelligent. The modern architect intends to gather together — and to this end even the systems of construction are changed to-day — the greatest possible number of advantages even in the smallest space ("comforts" it would be better to say if it were not a despised expression of the purists). However, just this makes the abolition of such an indispensable place absolutely incomprehensible; a place which, besides everything else, takes up no space, as it is possible to build it underneath the semi-basement. The man of good taste who has to buy a house to live in should demand a cellar, and it would be a good thing if every tenant refused to live in a house without one.

Our friend the wine lives in the cellar, rejoices and suffers there, acquires a flavour or depreciates, according to the care, the treatment, the "comforts" — may I be forgiven! — which we have afforded it.

Therefore the cellar must be well and carefully built; it should help to remember that, even if perfectly constructed, it will not be too expensive. I could add that we could even economise, for insuperable financial reasons, in the building and furnishing of a modern kitchen (reluctantly!); not, however, for a cellar: insuperable financial reasons do not exist.

I shall therefore limit myself to a few pieces of advice. First of all the cellar should face North because here there are less sudden changes of temperature. This is important because the wine needs an almost constant one. Remember that it should never fall below 48.2 degrees F., and never rise above 64.4 degrees.

We know that wine lives and, just because it lives, we have seen that it is susceptible to temperature. Apart from that, it hates, as we do, humidity. On account of this, it is necessary to study the insulation and, above all, to see that the level of the underground water is not such as to imperil the cellar continuously.

It is very important to take great care in preventing odours and smells from reaching the wine, as it absorbs them easily. The cellar should not, therefore, be adjoining the refuse dump, the stables, the manure heap, or anything else which emanates smells. Perfumes also harm wine naturally, even the best, the most delicate, confirming, as the poet sang, that there is no perfume to equal the goodness of that of the wine.

Take care that the cellar be situated in a very peaceful place. Vibrations are harmful to wine. It would be good if it could rest far from street traffic and railway tracks.

As we have said, wine hates humidity, the despicable product of the enemy water; therefore there must be the maximum ventilation and we shall have prevented the formation of mould. The windows, however, should be furnished with shutters which keep out the sun's rays. Wine loves the half-light, as if this were more favourable to its ancient meditations.

On all sides of the cellar there must be shelves fit for storing the bottles, bearing in mind that, according to the quality, some bottles like to remain softly lying down, some firmly upright and others, even if more rarely, in a slanting position. The suggestions of the producer must be followed very carefully.

May no work disturb its rest, no extraneous material its

regal meditation. If you are in the habit of collecting rags, paper, and junk, remember the attic, and if you have no attic (architects are capable of everything), give up the collection. Unless you want to give up the wine. Everything is possible, since wine is permissible to the man of good spirit and forbidden to the dull-witted. However, even should you be dull-witted, do not give up the cellar for this; sons do not always resemble their fathers.

In any case, when the cursed soul of an architect advises you to build a house without a cellar, think of the German poet, Hans Barth who, every Spring, came on a pilgrimage to the Italian cellars from Verona to Capri and wrote a very jocular spiritual guide about them.

Therefore build yourselves an ample, spacious, well-ventilated cellar, cheered by many beautiful bottles, some upright, some lying down, to contemplate with a friendly eye in the Spring, Summer, Winter and Autumn evenings, smiling contemptuously at the thought of "that man without song, without sound, without women and without wine, who should live a decade longer than you".

Wine-tasting

In order to judge and appreciate a wine, it must be tasted.

The taster "judges" it through the so-called organoleptic examination, which requires the association of sight, sense of smell and taste.

The gourmet appreciates it through a ceremony which, apart from a dish which brings out its quality, needs a careful setting in order to be perfect: beauty of the prepared table, fine glasses, good choice of flowers without perfume, the presence of gracious women, good conversation. In such a ceremony, the way in which the wine is served has a fundamental importance.

The Organoleptic Examination

First of all it is necesary to taste the wine in different seasons. Being, as we have seen, something alive, it modifies and changes continuously; it undergoes an evolution, passing through youth, maturity and old age at varying speeds of slowness according to the relationship between the numerous components and the surrounding conditions. Only with successive tastings, therefore, can one form a valid judgement.

The aphorism that one looks at wine, one breathes it, one tastes it and finally one talks about it is well known. Some people even affirm that the tasting should begin with music because of the delicate sound of wine being poured out.

Let us leave this last refinement to the French, even if I like to recall, through Goldoni's testimony, a strange instrument of Venetian invention: "a glass bottle, one foot high, in which there were many balls of different sizes, divided by small tubes, and which ended in a long neck convenient for putting into the mouth, through which the balls let out the liquor. The bottom of this bottle, called 'glo-glo', was filled; then, by putting it to one's mouth and raising one's elbow, the wine passed over the balls and the tubes and made a harmonious sound; when all the guests did this at the same time, the multiple sounds made a new and charming concerto".

As we are not concerned with such music, however, we will begin our examination through our sight.

Wine-tasting, as does love, begins through the eyes.

In front of his glass of wine, half-filled for a reason which we will discover later, the good drinker concentrates, then picks it up and lifts it to eye-level. Now he must judge the colour and the clarity, that is, in one word which is more fit to define the visual impression, the "appearance". And what appearance.

The chromatic scale of wines is practically infinite. We will limit ourselves to a few simple examples just in order to understand each other.

For white wines:
 watery white, almost colourless like water
 greenish white
 very pale straw
 pale straw with greenish reflections

VECCHI CASTELLI ROMANI

DRY RED WINE

PRODUCED AND BOTTLED IN ITALY BY

SANTARELLI

ROMA

Net Contents 24 Fl. Ozs.   Alcohol 12% by Volume

3 santirosa

dry rosè wine

PRODUCED AND BOTTLED IN ITALY BY

ROMA SANTARELLI S. P. A.

NET CONTENTS 24 FL. OZS. ALCOHOL 12 % BY VOLUME

LANUVIO

WHITE WINE

ALCOHOL 12°/o BY VOLUME

PRODUCED AND BOTTLED IN ITALY BY

SANTARELLI

ROMA   ROMA

NET CONTENTS: 1 PT. 8 FL. OZS.

Valle Vermiglia

FRASCATI CLASSICO

White Wine

PRODUZIONE CAMPILLI

NET CONTENTS 1 PT. 8 FL. OZS.
ALCOHOL 12% BY VOLUME

PRODUCED AND BOTTLED BY

AZIENDA AGRICOLA **VALLE VERMIGLIA** FRASCATI (ITALY)

deep straw, of varying deepness
golden yellow
amber

The reddish yellow, brown and blackish colours distinguish the white wines which are ill or oxidated.

For rosé wines:
pink like rose petals
cherry colour like cherries
claret colour, like cherries but darker

For red wines, with varying intensity and brightness:
ruby red
garnet red
purple red
violet red
brick red
orange

Negative colours: bluish red (typical of adulterated wines) and yellowish red (typical of over-mature wines).

For judgement of the colour, which will be favourable if true and distinct, some people prefer, particularly for red wines, the classical silver cup instead of a glass.

There is no doubt however when it comes to judging the clarity: a glass of colourless, pure crystal, clean and well-dried.

Simple observation by holding it up to the light is generally not enough. The good taster will carry out the examination after having put the glass between the eye and a not excessively bright light (a weak electric bulb, for example) and will slowly move the glass better to see any possible floating particles.

The descending scale is as follows:
shiny, when the wine is brighter than crystal

brilliant, when the wine has crystal transparency
very limpid
limpid

and, unfortunately, sometimes negative qualities: opaque, dull, opalescent, cloudy, full of lees.

Other elements of the visual examination are fluidity and smoothness and the sparkle or froth; the latter is particularly important because it helps to determine the genuineness and the place of origin of many wines. It can be (apart from the quality of the colour): evanescent and transient or persistent; with coarse or fine bubbles.

The aroma of the wine, due to all the volatile substances which emanate, is judged by the sense of smell (for this particular examination, it is advisable to have the wine slightly warm).

The good taster now slightly rotates his glass, making the liquid caress the sides. Apart from augmenting the vinous surface, this "dance" in contact with the air facilitates the emanation and frees the bouquet. It is a matter of seconds and the good taster is already breathing it deeply.

The feelings which he collects are:

the aroma, given to the wine by the characteristics of the grapes from which it is made;

the perfume, which is the smell acquired automatically during the rapid fermentation in the vat and then, little by little, with the slow changes of maturation.

The combination of all the olfactory sensations of a wine is called the "bouquet" (a French word meaning a bunch of flowers).

Generally, when the aroma lessens, with time the perfume becomes stronger, first in the barrel and then in the bottle. In fact, with regard to young wines, one can speak of smell rather than perfume which, in a wine of good quality, changes with the continuous and slow transformation of the maturing to a light

34

and penetrating fragrance. When the odour of a wine reminds one of ripe fruit, it is called "fruity"; when it is particularly characteristic, "sui generis".

Many people do not attach the importance it deserves to the olfactory examination; of course, they are mistaken: the perfumes which come from a great wine are a subtle pleasure. Unfortunately, of all the senses that of smell is the least trained, because our civilisation feels less and less the necessity to use it. Most people, therefore, do not have the so-called olfactory memory. This lack deprives them of one of the most positive aspects of wine-tasting.

In fact the perfume always changes from wine to wine, it even changes in the same type of wine which is produced from vines cultivated in different places. It is well-known that the vine of an aromatic wine, for example, transplanted from its classic earth to another of different composition or exposure, gives a wine with a diminished or modified aroma, at times without even a trace of the original one. It is just as wel known that the Barbera, cultivated in the classical zone of the Barolo and Barbaresco, acquires, even if lightly, some of the qualities of their perfumes.

One piece of useful advice for understanding the bouquet of a wine is only to half-fill the glass. It is understood better. It is an experience which has been proved in a thousand schools of oenology. Without the taster being aware of it, half fill one glass with wine and fill another with the same wine to the brim. The wine in the first glass will be judged the better.

The descending scale of the perfume is as follows:
full
noble
pronounced
delicate
subtle
light
evasive

There are naturally unpleasant odours too, due either to illness of the grapes and of the wine or to the bad condition of the barrels and bottles, but now is not the moment to discuss them. It is enough to remember the very frequent "cork smell".

Once the appearance and the bouquet have been judged, a good taster does not drink his wine. He takes a drop, passes it over his tongue and palate, then to this lips. Then, pursing his lips like a ... cul de poule, as the French say, he breathes some air which gathers all the aromas, fills his palate and reveals the most intimate secrets. To listen to them, to take from them every detail is an art for which constant experience is more valuable than a natural tendency.

Three types of sensations are felt: regarding taste, touch and temperature.

Oenologists have gradually formed a precise terminology of which I give the most used expressions, excluding those which are immediately understandable, such as "acid" or "sweet".

Abboccato - describes a wine in wihch a sweet taste is present.

Amabile - describes a wine in which a sweet taste in discernible.

Ammandorlato - describes a wine in which the sweet taste is perfectly blended with the bitter one.

Armonico - describes a wine in which the flavours merge together and heighten one another.

Asciutto - describes a completely fermented wine, but with a minimum of sugar content.

Astringente - describes a wine in which is detected, through excess tannin, sharpness and roughness.

Austero - quality of great wines when young, whose softness is interrupted by a light astringent taste.

Caldo - pleasing thermic sensation given by a wine of high alcohol and glycerine content.

Con fondo - Describes a wine in which a different taste is added to the fundamental one.

Con retrogusto - describes a wine which, as soon as it is drunk, leaves a new, different taste in the mouth.

Di corpo - describes a wine which has body, generally on account of a high alcohol content.

Erbaceo - describes an acidulous taste which recalls a flavour of grass.

Franco - describes a wine which has no after-taste.

Fresco - describes a wine which gives a feeling of freshness.

Fruttato - describes a wine which has the taste of ripe fruit.

Grasso - describes a wine which fills the mouth, flexible and generous.

Morbido - describes a pleasing tactile sensation, like a caress on a smooth surface.

Nervoso - describes a pleasing tactile sensation in which the softness is enriched by vivacity and liveliness.

Netto - describes a wine in wihch the basic taste (dry, sweet, etc.) is particularly pronounced.

Neutro - describes a wine with no predominating flavour.

Oleoso - describes a wine which is soft and smooth at the same time.

Passante - describes a wine which is not rough, which is flexible and does not jolt the palate.

Pastoso - the sweet taste is pronounced but does not dominate the others.

Pieno - describes a wine which has richness and body.

Rotondo - describes a wine which is full and, at the same time, soft.

Ruvido - describes a wine which produces a rasping sensation on the tongue.

Sapido - of alive and full taste.

Stoffa - a quality of great wines. which, during the tasting, fill the mouth and seem to acquire a new dimension and a new volume.

Sulla vena - describes a wine in which the sweet taste is felt.

Vellutato - of a pleasant tactile sensation, like stroking velvet. To give a better definition it is easier to tell an anecdote. A glass of Gattinara was offered to a poor countryman in order to experiment "in anima vili", that is, on a very simple subject. "Well, my friend, what is your impression? what do you think of it?" the oaf was asked. "Ah, dear Sirs", he replied coming out, as it were, of a sort of ecstasy, "it seems to me that God is descending ... in velvet trousers".

Vinoso - of a sound and genuine taste

Serving the wine

How many times have you heard it said "there's no accounting for tastes"? Innumerable times. Yet there is no sadder phrase. All of you will agree with me that a pair of yellow shoes with a blue suit leaves no doubt.

It is true that between good and bad taste there are endless degrees. I will tell you the rules for appreciating wine according to good taste, rules which contrast very strongly with the standards established by unqualified people.

I hope you have a rich and relaxing cellar or, after having read my catalogue, you are stocking it, finding the wines, one by one, from qualified producers.

I will therefore say only a few words for those who, for any reason whatsoever, should go to the nearest wine merchant.

First of all: make sure that he has a large cellar and not only the four walls of his shop. Secondly: refuse the bottles which have been in the window or on the shelves, exposed to light and noise, probably upright.

Should a wine arrive just at that moment from a friend instead, remember that it is better to drink it immediately than after two or three days, because the effects of the journey become more accentuated after the first hours of repose. The best thing to do, and I am sure you will want only the best after reading these pages, is to let it rest for about ten days, away from the light, vibration and noise.

If, in the end, you choose your wine at your leisure and responsibility, from your cellar, be careful of the transportation. The short journey from the cellar to the table is sufficient to ruin a great wine. Transfer the bottle with great care, holding it at the same angle as it was before, in a small wicker basket, without shaking it, without bumping it, without swinging it, until arriving at the table. The basket, called "cradle", must be of such a form that the bottle rests there, lying down, with the top slightly higher than the centre of the bottom.

If you do not wish to use the basket, you must remember to put the bottles upright... a month before drinking them, if one wants to be meticulous; well, let us say at least 24 hours.

Every wine has to be drunk at its own temperature which you may now find under each description. I will therefore dedicate only a few lines to this subject.

It is one thing to carry out an organoleptic examination by tasting it, and another to drink it with affectionate care.

Some people have wanted to transfer the norms of wine-tasting into the field of food. To be coherent, one should therefore change the meal into a concert, other than Goldoni's instrument, of suckings, garglings and bangings. This would not only render it disgusting or ridiculous but also prevent the development of the meal.

I have thus perfectly understood that, for the organoleptic examination, certain sweet white wines can and must be drunk only at one or two degrees below room temperature; I deny that they should be drunk at the end of a meal when, because of the natural consumption of food, one is already satiated with calories.

I only drink the lighter wines of low alcohol content cool,

and some are really very pleasant, and Muscat wines on account of their natural delicacy.

The ideal temperature for savouring an average white wine is, however, 50 degrees F. Below this the aroma and the perfume are not developed enough; above it, they are accentuated but the taste is completely distorted.

Good white vintage wines need to be drunk at 46.4 degrees F.; this temperature moderates their exuberant richness, but reveals all their subtle harmony, while a more intense cold would annul their qualities or hide them.

But the great white wines, dessert or sweet ones, alcoholic ones, full-bodied ones (on account of their not only exuberant but also excessive richness, that intimidates the weak men of to-day — and so true is this fact that consumption has decreased too much) require an inferior temperature, 42.8 or even 41.0 degrees F., which allows their magnificent values and qualities to be felt, without being suffocated. Their aroma, their perfume are such that they will satisfy us just as much.

Sparkling wines are drunk at the same temperature, or rather if they are very dry (brut is the exact term) at even two degrees lower.

White or dry Vermouth is also served extremely cold (39.2-41.0 degrees F.) and very cold (42.8-44.6 degrees F.) if it is sweet. Red Vermouth is served cool.

To bring a white wine down to a low temperature it is best, whenever possible, to use natural methods; in Winter, by exposing the bottle to the open air. In many hilly areas, on many estates, there still exist grottoes dug according to the experience of the past generations, in which, depending on the locality, the bottles are brought to the right degree of coldness.

In the absence of natural means, either the classical bucket filled with finely crushed ice or the refrigerator must be used; in the case of the latter, use the least cold part, the cold part and, only in some cases, the freezer (not, however, before having put the wine in the other two parts first), as necessary.

It takes ten minutes to chill a bottle which is immersed in

a bucket, twenty to make it cold and at least half an hour to bring it down to a few degrees above freezing point.

Attention: it must be taken into account that wine served at 46.4 degrees F. will arrive at 50-53.6 degrees in just over ten minutes.

To cool wine by putting in it pieces of ice which destroy it, breaking it and watering it down, is to be excluded and is considered barbaric. In fact it is advisable to remember that, even though every wine has a water content of 85-90%, it is not possible to dilute even a very alcoholic wine with even a very small quantity of water. The taste would immediately reveal it, on account of a break in the constitution of the wine (which does not occur when, for instance, a very alcoholic wine is blended with one containing less alcohol). The water in the wine, as we have already said, is born of the wine, it has a metabolic origin and therefore has something alive in itself, something personal, which, pure as it is, ordinary water could never have. It is for this reason that the water in the wine is called "vitalised".

It is another story altogether for red wines. Here, the more the temperature rises, within limits of course, the more the wines are "discovered" and the qualities and defects are accentuated, exactly contrary to the white wines.

The full-bodied red wines, therefore, shall be drunk at slightly above room temperature (conventionally established at 64.4 degrees F.) up to 68-71.6 degrees F., descending also to 57.2 degrees F. for certain wines with no body which should be drunk cool, in order to deceive us and to be swallowed without being noticed.

The season is also important: in the hot months, I will allow you two or four degrees less.

Certainly the right temperature of a wine is important. It was after having drunk Procanico at room temperature that someone affirmed it did not deserve the praise it was given. He would have had the same delusion had he drunk Gattinara fresh.

In order to bring red wines to their average temperature, it is enough to keep them 48 hours in a place where the temperature is constantly about 64.4 degrees F. It they are wanted a few degrees higher, keep them in the kitchen not too far from the stove. Avoid, however, sudden warming, too near a source of direct heat or in hot water, which is sometimes resorted to forgetting that wine is extremely sensitive to sudden changes of temperature. If anything, use tepid water. A red wine treated too brusquely could break (se casser, as the French say) like a sparkling wine put directly into the freezer.

If the wine does not reach the temperature required, it can be obtained by holding the glass between the palms of the hands.

One last piece of advice for those who adore perfection: heat the glasses if the wine is to be served at 71.6 degrees F.; frost them if it is to be served very cold.

The bottles of full-bodied red wines are uncorked 24 hours before drinking them. In Piedmont it is the custom to keep " 'l fund 'd buta" (that which remains in a bottle uncorked the previous day) for the guest of honour, as it is considered the best. It is indispensable to uncork any bottle of red wine 2 hours before drinking so that it loses that "closed" smell, which a sensitive palate would detect immediately. For rosé and white wine, ½ an hour is sufficient.

The only exceptions are perl wines and sparkling wines which are uncorked at the moment of serving.

It is not as simple as it seems to uncork a bottle. Here is the correct way:

Remove the top part of the metal capsule, cutting it ¼ inch beneath the rim of the bottle (where the glass usually forms a band) so that, when the wine is poured out, it will encounter no obstacle;

clean the top of the bottle, above all where it has been in contact with the cork, and, keeping it steady with the left hand, insert the corkscrew (the type with a wide thread-pitch which, by simply turning a handle or pushing down two levers, extracts the cork; never the T-shaped type) straight in the centre and screw it to the bottom of the cork (if you are sure it has taken well) but not far enough to pass right through; then extract it;

clean the bottle again;

smell the cork because if it smells bad it is almost certain that the contents of the bottle have a bad taste; in which case, taste the wine before serving it.

The guests already being at table, it should be remembered that a little wine is poured into the host's glass first. Once the wine has been approved by him, serve the guests, leaving the host till last.

The wine is poured out by resting the bottle on the edge of the glass, letting it run out smoothly. To avoid drops falling on the table, it is sufficient to raise the bottle gently, turning it on its own axis.

It may happen, particularly with great red vintage wines, that the bottle contains such a large quantity of sediment that it is impossible to serve it, even in the cradle, without provoking a disaster. One must therefore resort to the so-called decanting.

Take a decanter of crystal transparency and a candle.

Put the decanter on the table and place the candle behind it. With the right hand, raise the bottle (which you have already kept upright for 48 hours) and slowly lean the top on the edge of the decanter. Let the wine run out as slowly as possible but without interruptions. The flame of the candle will show up the transparency of the wine. As soon as the wine begins to appear dull, be careful and, immediately the sediment is seen, end the operation by lifting up the bottle. Finish emptying it in a separate glass.

Decanting has not only the advantage of maintaining limpidity. It totally eliminates the so-called "closed" smell, revives the bouquet, re-establishes the wine as a whole and gathers it in a carafe (which is chambrée) particularly suitable on account of its crystal transparency for showing up its appearance.

When serving in the decanter, do not forget to present the memorable, dusty bottle to the guests. Not out of vanity — even be it legitimate — but out of a dutiful sense of recognition and respect. To decant wine in a carafe is like preparing it for its grand entrance into society.

There remain the glasses to be talked about. I shall be indulgent; choose them according to your own tastes as long as you respect these conditions: that they have a base and a stem; that they be absolutely transparent, shiny and colourless, with fine crystalline sides, unground, without facets, angles, thickenings and ornamental motive whatsoever. It is better that the diameter narrow a little, very little, towards the rim, in order to gather the bouquet better. Therefore, no tulip-shaped glasses.

They should not be too small, especially if they must contain good wines. Remember Offenbach's protest:

> That which I can never explain to myself:
> in Paris why does one drink
> bad wine in big glasses and
> good wine in small ones?

By this I do not say that the glass of Henry II, which he had modelled on the breast of Diana of Poitiers and which is admired still to-day at Poitiers Castle, was ideal even if it were made of crystal. They were times, lucky they, of other breasts and other tastes.

And now, how are wines drunk? Do not make me repeat it. It is simple; adopting all those rules of tasting which do not clash with good manners.

Above all, however, drink it with love.

Wines, like beautiful women, are different, mysterious and fickle. Every wine, like a woman, has to be conquered.

It always begins by refusing, either politely or rudely according to its temperament, and it concedes only to him who aspires to its soul as well as to its body. It will belong only to him who knows how to "discover" it with gentleness.

Would you like some Rabelaisian analogies? The legendary bosom of Jane of Aragon — too veiled in the paintings of Raphael and Leonardo — emanated a subtle and disturbing perfume of ripe peaches (suavissimo fragrantes odore persicis pomis persimiles redolent), exactly like the best Sylvaner of the Alto Adige.

Verdicchio

DEI CASTELLI DI JESI

vino secco pregiato

ditta STAPHILUS

BARTELUCCI & FANTONE·ANCONA·

G. C. V.

VINI DEL TRENTINO

№ 92362

MARZEMINO

PRODUCED & BOTTLED IN ITALY BY

Grande
cantina
viticoltori
Soc. Coop. a r l.
Trento

CONSORZIO
CANTINE SOCIALI
DEL TRENTINO

FRASCATI

Fine *Wine*

PRODUCED AND BOTTLED IN ITALY BY

SANTARELLI S.p.A.

ROMA

NET CONTENTS 24 FL. OZS. ALCOHOL 12 % BY VOLUME

Jean-Baptiste Siméon Chardin: La nappe

Wine and food

A table without wine
is an organ without bellows
a woman without hair
a family without children.

One reads this — or one used to — written on a wall in an inn in Parenzo.

The Istrian poet is right: sad is the table without wine. Wine exalts the taste of food and spiritualizes it. In its turn, the taste of the food favours the development of the bouquet and of the wine's other qualities.

In order that this should happen, it is necessary that the wine and the food be judiciously married, that it be a marriage of love and not of convenience. The combination of such marriages is more difficult than at first appears; the history, the task and the personality of him who makes the choice all come together.

To each type of food therefore its own wine; but this is not enough; it is also necessary to know how to harmonize the sequence of wines as it is to harmonize that of courses. Generally, very generally, speaking, thus: make the strongest most full bodied wines follow the lightest and most delicate; serve white wines at the beginning and at the end of the meal, avoiding one white wine following another.

May what I have said convince you to take no notice of the fable that wines of different colours and qualities, one on top of the other, make you drunk, or worse. If this happens, it is because, by changing wines, you are apt to drink more: just be careful.

Nor is it true, indeed it is ridiculous, that red wines are superior to white ones (as would also be the contrary).

> Also St. Peter said, "That red wine is better"
> and St. Peter was right
> because that red wine is certainly better.

This is a little song, which, sung in an inn in front of a beautiful glass of red wine, could even be pleasant, but above all it shows that St. Peter was no gastronome.

The fashion of despising sweet wines, whoever wishes to do so, is just as ridiculous. A Chambave wine of Val d'Aosta, whose grapes have been harvested in a warm Autumn and whose bunches have been selected one by one, wonderfully accompanies little cakes with which an austere Barolo would be detestable. On the other hand a Picolit, drunk with a shoulder of pork, would be dishonoured.

Be it red or white wine it must be pure. Water is used for many wonderful purposes, but at table only for one. When changing bottles it is, in fact, advisable to take a sip (I said "a sip") of cold water. Being in the mood for popular quotations, I will give you one last little Venetian poem, even if the original is in Latin, from which it has been translated word for word:

> *The first glass is pure*
> *the second is hard*
> *the third is waterless*
> *the fourth pagan*
> *the fifth as God gives it*
> *and the others like the first.*

One more word before passing on to gastronomic combinations. I have never understood why wine, if we exclude the Vermouths, is not served as an aperitif in Italy. A Nasco, to take only one example, served cold, very cold, almost iced, is just as good as any. Never has any bar offered me the same abandoned pleasure as that most noble cave, in Florence, where open sandwiches of cheese, nuts and olives are brought with the wine (and another common saying: the bitterness of the olive is a balsam to the wine).

I could easily write a whole book on the marriages between food and wines. I shall limit myself, both because of space and in order not to deprive you of the subtle pleasure of choosing, to giving you some indication, in general terms, which does not and should not be dictatorial. There are many exceptions (nearly always very pleasant), whose discovery will bring you rightful joy.

If you can, I would advise you not to take away the wine glasses together with the food for which they were intended. It could happen, as it has happened many times to me, that you find, for example, a Barbaresco, estimated and proved excellent with veal cutlets Pojarsky, absolutely oustanding with foie-gras à la Strasbourg which follows.

I am perfectly aware that this is in contrast to the regulations of service and to traditional basic rules, but I have always believed that a little fantasy, upheld by certain taste, does not spoil anything.

One last piece of advice: if you are travelling, "force" your fantasy. It is amazing how the cuisine in each place matches the local wines in the most unpredictable and audacious combinations.

Sea food hors d'oeuvres. Light, dry wines (e.g. Soave, Lugana, Polcevera).

Meat and vegetable hors d'oeuvres. Dry or sweet rosé wines, such as Chiaretto del Garda and Rosato del Salento. If the hors d'oeuvres, also those of sea food, are flavoured with vinegar or lemon sauces, no wine is advisable.

Pickles. No wine.

Oysters and sea food. Oysters without wine is a body without a soul. This time the principle is undisputable; sea food requires great dry, indeed very dry, white wines, but with not too much body and fairly young; there is nothing wrong if they are brightened with a sour touch (e.g. Vernaccia di Oristano).

Consommé. If they contain a slight flavouring of great wines no wine; if they are without, sweet rosé and red wines.

Thick soups. White wines, either dry, or sweetish, or demi-sweet, and rosé wines, either dry or sweetish (e.g., among the white ones, Tocai and Verduzzo; among the rosé ones, Castel del Monte rosato and Cerasuolo degli Abruzzi).

Pasta and risotto dishes. The sauce which accompanies them determines the wine. If it has a fish base, dry white wines; if it has a meat base, dry, light red wines; if it has a game base, robust red wines.

Egg dishes. Fresh, dry white wines (e.g. Bianco Secco dell'Oltrepò and Gambellara).

Fish. Dry, white wines of average body (Coronata, Valchiana, Verdicchio, Vermentino, etc.).

Fine fish. If cooked simply (roast, grilled, etc.) great dry white wines such as Malvasia di Cagliari and Vernaccia di San Gimignano. If prepared with sauces, white such as Orvieto "abboccato".

Fish soup. Sweetish and velvety white wines (Albana, Colonna, etc.).

White meat roasts. Soft red wines of average body such as Barbaresco, Carema, and Ghemme.

Red meat roasts. Austere red wines, of good body, such as the classical Chianti, Montecarlo Rosso and Vino Nobile di Montepulciano.

Boiled meats and stews. Full bodied and young wines (e.g. Barbera).

Fowl. Light, aromatic and dry red wines (Bardolino, Castelli di Mezzacorona, Grignolino, etc.).

Game. Aromatic, full-bodied red wines (e.g. Brunello, Carmignano, Gattinara). Strong tasting and aromatic red wines, very full-bodied, such as Recioto Amarone and Taurasi.

Foie gras. If tinned: dry sparkling wines or sweet wines of excellent quality, such as the very alcoholic Moscadello di Montalcino and Picolit. If fresh: dry red wines of good body, whose place of origin is certain (Barbaresco, Brunello, etc.).

Salads. No wine.

Vegetables. The wines are determined by the food which accompanies them.

Cheeses. Very generally speaking, with fresh and mild cheeses, wines of average body; with strong cheeses, dry or semi-dry alcoholic wines or dry sparkling wines (but each type of cheese requires a special choice).

Sweets. Sweet and sweetish sparkling wines or sweet and very sweet fresh white wines (Asti Spumante, Cartizze, Spumante, Malvasia del Vulture, Moscati, etc.).

Ice cream. No wine.

Fruit. If not preceded by a sweet: sweet, delicately sweet white and rosé wines such as the sweet Greco di Tufo, Ravello Rosato. Il preceded by a sweet, very alcoholic dessert wines, such as Canonau di Cagliari, Moscato di Pantelleria, Nasco. Remember that citrus fruits refuse any wine whatsoever.

If you really wish, wine may be drunk even when the meal is over, and away from the table. Skimming through these pages, you will find more than a few such types. However, remember not to imitate that Milanese count who played patience every evening in front of numerous bottles. As, playing alone, he always won, he condemned the bottles to pay him something to drink. That count was a drunkard.

All the same, he had a certain spirit: he used to trim his Virginian cigars very diligently, one by one, and put them in a glass of rough brandy; he sucked through them until he tasted the brandy which soaked the cigar. He then put them to dry, and having dried thoroughly, he smoked them impregnated with that perfume.

Liqueurs

While wine, pagan and pantheistic, may be considerd divine fruit, if not a God himself as the classical and Biblical legend tells us, alcohol, Satanic and conventual, is without doubt fruit of Man. With the coming of Christianity and after the purifying bath from barbarity, Man threw himself into the feverish search for something new which would again make him equal to or at least near the Gods: the elixir of long life, the coveted philtre which repulses death, certain recognition of his subjection, as far as possible... to infinity. And here are the magic formulas, and here is the elixir of the Count of Cagliostro, the potion of star-water, potable gold. We are in the era when the most enlightened minds condemned the sacrilegious attempts, defined by Petrarca as "smoke, ashes, sweat, sighs, words, deceits, abuse" and of Dante confining the contrivers in the bowels of his Inferno.

But nothing of Man or of his attempts is destined to die without leaving a sign: to the great discoveries and inventions (new continents, the press, the compass) we must add the spirit of the wine. The first authentic documents belong to the end of the 13th. century: the description of "aqua ardens" is found in "Liber Ignum" by Mario Greco and, in "De Conservanda Iuventute" by Arnaldo da Villanova, these words may be read: "A sort of burning wine is extracted for distillation and it is called brandy. It is the essence of the wine, it is the permanent water or rather water of gold. It prolongs the life and therefore deservers to be called 'aqua vitae' (water of life)". Arnaldo da Villanova thus established the baptism of brandy. Aqua vitae. The name in itself is exalting, the exciting flavours already exist together with the promising experiences and — alas! — the misleading hopes, water of life.

In the first half of the 15th. century, after laborious attempts, G.M. Savonarola initiated the modern art of liqueur-making, succeeding in combining the burning water with vegetable aromas and perfumes in a liquid called "aqua ardens composita". The first compound liqueur, in the modern sense.

Savonarola was also the name of the saintly and heretical monk; it is like a predestination. From that time onwards, as soon as the caves of magic disappeared (but only at the end of the 18th. century with the French Revolution did they disappear completely), alchemy... Satan was received into the monasteries. As in the preceding centuries there existed the cult of literature and art, now the stills of the alchemists were inherited, marking the first great development in the art of *liqueur-making*.

Satan is in the monastery: remember that good monk, liqueur-maker and sinner in one of Maupassant's stories (a subject which fascinated even France). Through tasting and tasting, through diligence, and for love of perfection, the alcohol of his distillations put an unrestrainable song in his heart. The monastery then resounded with libertine songs, which the good monks tried to cover up with psalmodic prayers.

The liqueurs entered not only the monastery but also the kitchen, and trimphantly; to-day we find them a necessary complement, as well as wine, for many good recipes, for cake-making and ice-cream-making. Caterina de' Medici, bride at the French Court, included among her attendants the men in charge of her liqueur stock. The Italian liqueurs, such as Ratafià, Rosolio and Vespetrò, therefore crossed the Alps and established themserves in the "sweet land".

Confirming Italy's supremacy, Louis XIV, who adored Rosolio, sent one of his "official tasters", a certain Audigier, to Italy with precise instructions to collect liqueur recipes. On his return, Audigier published a book ... and founded a factory.

A factory. Even a brief excursion into the history of liqueurs and brandies cannot be completed without mentioning the liqueur industry which has been gradually establishing itself, after the French Revolution, parallel with restaurants, cafés and later, bars. The first intelligent preoccupation if not of all, of many factories was to adapt the new mechanical and scientific inventions to an old and noble experience. These industries slowly expanded until they reached the complexes they are to-day.

Spirits

Gancia

VERMOUTH
ROSSO
DI TORINO
PROVVEDITORI DI S.M IL RE D'ITALIA DAL 1870

FRATELLI GANCIA & C.IA   LIC.N.9

CASA FONDATA NEL 1850 - SOC. AZ. VERMOUTH APERITIVI SPUMANTI S. p. A. - CANELLI (ITALIA)

We shall call spirits the products of direct distillation of the wines, of their by-products, the fruit and corn.

Brandy

It is a product of the distillation of more or less matured wine, without sugar and extraneous aromas having been added. Its goodness is derived directly from the quality of the wine used and through the method by which it is prepared (above all from a clean separation between the "head and tail", i.e., the so-called beginning and end of distillation and from the means and duration of ageing). Italy is a great producer of brandies (documents prove that, since the 14th. century, their commerce and export has existed in Modena). Among the many, we will cite the most famous from Ponte di Bassano and the two from Villacidro, in the province of Cagliari, a very dry white one and a highly aromatic yellow coloured one.

Juniper Berries brandy

This is obtained by distilling juniper berries. Quite a lot is produced in Italy although the foreign specialities, Steinhager and Gin, are better known. Italian juniper berry brandy is produced at Edolo, Abbadia Alpina, Asiago and Bagni di Porretta; the brandy of the latter place is poetically called "Rugiada di flora" (flower dew-drops).

Cherry brandy

This is prepared by distilling the fleshy cherries of the "prunus cerasus". Commercially it is called Kirsch. It is of foreign origin and produced abroad, but a good result is also obtained in the Alto Adige.

Plum brandy

It is obtained by distilling plums. The Slivovitz from Friuli is particularly appreciated. Pale blond colour, with an intense aroma and a very pleasant taste.

Gentian brandy

This is made by distilling gentians, which grow in abundance in the Italian mountains; those from Val Camonica, Val di Sole and Val di Fiemme are particularly appreciated.

Brandy

The spirit, obtained by distilling wine and which is mature, improved and aged, is called brandy.

Its value comes from all those volatile substances, either

brought out or not through analysis, which constitute the flavour, the perfume itself and, better still, the soul of the wine.

Grappa

The product obtained from the distillation of wine marc (the solids of the grape consisting mainly of skins and seeds) is called grappa. A precise preparation and the ageing in oak casks, according to the wise experience consolidated over the centuries, enable it to withstand many comparisons of delicacy and bouquet. In an anlysis, grappa, in comparison with brandy, has a higher content of aldehyde, esters and higher alcohols.

The strong peasant art has indulged its whims in the production of many types of good quality grappa. Grappa from Barolo, the light green and bitterish Grappa from Montalto, the types of Grappa from Val d'Aosta, Feltre, Bardolino, Bassano del Grappa, Carpi and from many, many other places are very famous. When leaving on his gastronomic tour, Paolo Monelli stated: "It seems to us necessary to settle the vexed question whether the Grappa from Mongiove is worth more than those from Feltre and from Bassano ". The severe examination of the relative texts contained in the "Wandering Glutton" brings me to the conclusion that they are equally good. This is what is written about the Grappa from Val d'Aosta: "It is a very shining grappa, bottled iced sun, pure and simple, without secondary flavours, without additional sweetening. Perfect." This is written about that from Feltre: "Years ago I wrote in great praise about the Grappa of Feltre, how it is succinct and perfect, how it gathers the ice from the mountain tops and the sun from the hills which sit looking towards the Tomatico mountain in the North; how it is drunk fresh, because its warmth is enclosed within, its virtue is hermetic, and its motto is 'ex gelu aestuat' ." Finally, about the Grappa from Bassano, are these words: "It will descend into the glass like a very limpid water, divine, to see under the light, as one does with precious stones, how it shines and glitters."

Liqueurs

The products from the blending and maceration of spirits, aromas and syrups are defined as liqueurs. Here I will consider only the typical Italian ones, established by a precise technique of production and long tradition.

Acqua di Fiume

A speciality of Villafranca near Verona. Whitish water colour, full aroma, sweet aromatic taste, alcohol by vol. 36%. Gabriele d'Annunzio wrote thus about it: "... is limpid and light like that which descends from the Carso river to soften the ardour of the Città Olocausta (Trieste)".

Alchermes

It is a traditional Italian speciality, produced since time immemorable in Florence by the monks of St. Maria Novella and by the Carthusian monks. It is made with alcohol, cinnamon, carnations, vanilla, coriander, nutmeg, scented with the essence of roses, jasmine, and orris roots, coloured with cochineal. The classical Alchermes, served in a bottle of pure crystal, sends out marvellous reflections onto the table, owing to its rich, clear and vivid carmine colour; reflections which seem to come from a liquefied ruby of delicate and brilliant transparency and incomparable splendour.

Alpestre

A speciality with a spirit base and a good 35 Alpine herbs, alcohol by vol. 50%, prepared by Maristi Fathers of Carmagnola.

Anice

It is distilled from aniseed, more or less aromatic. Italy has many types, from very diverse origins and of varying alcohol content. From the triduan Anesone of Solo and of Orzinuovi alcohol by vol. 40%, watery white colour, delicate taste, to the Anisetta of Ascoli; from the strong Anice of Trieste to the Anicione of Finale Emilia; from the Sambuca of Lazio to the Sassolino of Sassuolo.

Anthemis

Liqueur produced from aromatic herbs by the Benedictine monks of Montevergine. Light green colour, medium alcohol content, taste and aroma in which mint prevails.

Biferno

A liqueur from Bojano, in the province of Campobasso. Yellowy orange colour, sweet taste, alcohol by vol. 40%.

Centerbe

A speciality from Tocco Casauria in the Abruzzi, of ancient fame, with a high alcohol content and with the perfume of the hundreds of mountain herbs from the Gran Sasso mountain, a beautiful green colour. Paolo Monelli was enthusiastic about it: "By drinking this liquid precious stone, we make ourselves one with the great mountain, with all the massif of noble rock and the resplendent ice which rises to guard the heart of Italy. Centerbe, which means a hundred herbs, and all from the trembling meadows of the heights; from them is distilled an intense and pungent lymph, of very powerful aroma, which unleashes a gale in the mouth, penetrates the heart in a blizzard, and gathers together one's lost youth".

Cerasella di Fra Ginepro

A speciality of Pescara, with a base of spirit and aromas of fruit with a prevalence of wild cherries, alcohol by vol. 38%, bright ruby red colour.

Certosino

Antique conventual speciality from the Carthusian house at Monte Acuto. It is produced in both yellow and green colours, as is its sister-wine "Gratiarum Chartusia" from the Carthusian house at Pavia.

Corfinio

A liqueur of Chieti, medium alcohol content, pleasant taste.

Fior d'Agno

A liqueur of Valdagno. Reddish brown colour, pleasing, aromatic taste, in which vanilla is detected, alcohol by vol. 40%.

Fiordalpe

A sweet aromatic liqueur from the Italian Alps, pale colour. Its bottle contains a twig on which, when cold, the sugar forms white crystals of a very attractive appearance. At room temperature the sugar dissolves and falls to the bottom, leaving the twig bare but not harming the quality of the liqueur.

Ginepy

A speciality from the Val d'Aosta based on spirit and a sort of absinth from the Alps, of medium alcohol content, prepared in two types: one white and one green.

Maraschino

A liqueur which originates from Dalmatia; it enjoys world fame. It is prepared from the wild, black Morello cherry and retains all its perfume; the taste is very sweet, fine and delicate; alcohol by vol. 35%; white colour. It is excellent for the preparation of cocktails, exquisite in sour type cocktails instead of sugar, when a delicate suggestion of a different taste is required. Its use in cocktails is favoured on account of its excellent ability to mix with other fruit flavours.

Matese

Another speciality from Bojano. Mint green colour, dry taste, sour, alcohol by vol. 66%.

Menta

A liqueur with a base of spirit and small mint leaves. Italy boasts appreciated specialities: from the delicate Mentuccia di San Silvestro of Pavese (alcohol by vol. 42%, emerald green colour) to the icy Menta of Abbadia Alpina, to the Liquore di Menta of Pancalieri.

Mistrà

Whitish watery colour, bright; strictly dry taste of aniseed; alcohol by vol. 55%.

Nocillo

A liqueur of Acerra, in the province of Naples. Coffee colour, slightly bitter taste, pleasant, alcohol by vol. 45%.

Nocino

Speciality of Sassuolo and Luzzara in Emilia, produced by the infusion of tender nut husks in alcohol; it has an important gastronomic use, as it gives a very delicate aroma to ice-creams.

Poncio

A liqueur of Molise, perfumed by several aromas; orange, lemon, tangerine, and vanilla; alcohol by vol. 45%.

Vespetrò

Speciality of Canzo, in the province of Como. Golden yellow colour, aromatic taste, alcohol by vol. 43%.

Liqueur-tasting

I shall now discuss the tasting of brandies and liqueurs. For the latter, choose small glasses, with a stem, made of pure crystal; for the brandies, choose the classical brandy glass with a short stem, also of pure crystal. The real gentleman will not offer spirit in glasses which are different one from another and will discard inexorably coloured glass, even if it is Bohemian. Shame on the glass of metal or wood. The glasses are put on little plates covered with doilies. Generally liqueurs are served cold in glasses which are also cold; the brandies, warmed to room temperature, are served in glasses already heated.

Do not let yourselves be taken in by the usual phrases, "It's matter of opinion... all variations are legitimate... there's no accounting for tastes"; maybe, but he who has it, this stricly educated taste, to drink liqueurs and brandies, which are real and true flora of colours and tastes, observes rigid and precise rules. Liqueurs must be served immediately before coffee, and the brandies a reasonable time afterwards. It is a principle which we are not the first to proclaim.

At the end of a meal, no person of good taste would renounce, for any reason whatsoever, tasting, before the coffee, a classical liqueur, very slowly in long moments of abandonment, just as no intelligent lady would serve a rough brandy, even a very old "ron", during a bridge or canasta party. The card-playing would be disturbed, whereas the soft smoothness of a cordial would help it.

And which refined gallant will deny himself the scoundrel's joy of offering a liqueur to his enchanting companion?

In liqueurs, women find a comparison with their own sweetness, sharpened by a thousand little games of their enchanting lips. Their faces glow under their maquillage, their eyes brighten... with the desire to quicken the docile sensuality of their fresh and radiant skin. For liqueurs bring to the surface their loving disposition.

They must be drunk cold, savouring them, first caressed by the eyes, then by the lips, the tongue, without violence, without hurry, in minute sips, like something rare, precious, which a quick swallow would brutally destroy. The refined person will alternate sips of liqueur with a little iced water.

At a reasonable time after the coffee, a good brandy, a grappa or a Slivovitz from Friuli will be served at room temperature — with only one of two exceptions — in small brandy glasses which have already been warmed. A brandy should not be drunk but only sipped. Contemplate the colour which will be brought out by the pure crystal of the glass, warmed by the gentle heat of your hand. Breathe in the perfume deeply in order to gather the initial most delicate and most volatile aromas; closing the eyes, let some drops run into the mouth. Continue to warm them there: the brandy expands, dissolves and disappears. It will provoke an intense delight through long, enchanting moments. Only then will the mysterious liquid disclose all its secrets.

In many countries, especially the Scandinavian ones, Russia and the United States of America, a greater quantity of alcohol is drunk than in Italy; this is due to the fact that we do not

VINO D'ORIGINE

LA MIA CANTINA

CARTIZZE

• ACQUI •

VINO D'ORIGINE

LA MIA CANTINA

CARTIZZE

• ACQUI •

TENUTA S. MARGHERITA

FERMENTAZIONE   NATURALE

PROSECCO

FRIZZANTE AMABILE

Cantine S. Margherita
Fondiaria Agricola Ind. s.p.a.
Villanova di Portogruaro

ALCOOL 12% COMPL. CA.   CONT. CC. 730 CA.

VINO D'ORIGINE

LA MIA CANTINA

PINOT GRIGIO

• ACQUI •

Gancia

aperitivo

Gancia rosso

FRATELLI GANCIA & C.ᴵᴬ

SOC. AZ. VERMOUTH APERITIVI SPUMANTI S. p. A. CANELLI (Italia)

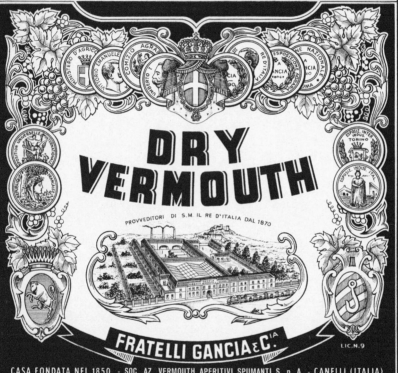

Gancia

DRY VERMOUTH

PROVVEDITORI DI S.M. IL RE D'ITALIA DAL 1870

FRATELLI GANCIA & C.ᴵᴬ

LIC. N. 9

CASA FONDATA NEL 1850 - SOC. AZ. VERMOUTH APERITIVI SPUMANTI S. p. A. - CANELLI (ITALIA)

LA GRAFICA - TORINO

swallow alcohol, but we enjoy it slowly. Liqueurs are worth nothing for their alcohol itself, but for the aromas dissolved in this alcohol.

It is improbable that an authentic gastronome will drink two glasses — even if it be of the best. And here a digression is permitted: the host should not insist too much in offering. This for many reasons, but also in order not to imitate that Monsu Tasca, legendary among the perambulatory wine-merchants of Turin who, having stopped for a while in Piazza della Legna and other places, wandered through Via Roma at night with his little cart. Meeting a possible client, he would present him with a glass of liqueur; if it were refused, the merchant, half-closing his eyes, would gulp it down, exlaiming, "Don't you want it? I'll drink it myself then!" And he would smile, blowing out his cheeks, which burnt from the heat of the grappa. The following sestina was very popular at that time:

> Hello Monsu Tasca,
> Come down here,
> Give me a small glass
> Of my favourite brandy;
> Give me some very strong brandy,
> Which will help my digestion.

On the other hand, do not be slaves of prejudice. A good liqueur, if drunk in moderation, does good and does not harm.

While studying at school, it so happened that the Dean had a notice hung up with this intimidating inscription: "ALCOHOL POISONS, ALCOHOL KILLS!" A humourist completed these wise words by adding: "YES, FATHER, ALCOHOL POISONS, ALCOHOL KILLS! BUT IT TAKES TIME!"

Conclusion

There we are, I have done. I think I have given you a sufficiently complete list of the Italian wines. It is up to you now to get to know them better, more intimately... by drinking them.

It is now possible for you to buy a good wine unhesitatingly, or almost. Leaving modesty aside, I believe that it is I who have made this possible with my catalogue which gives the places of production of every wine even indicating the best places of origin.

It will be sufficient that we take a little trouble over persuading our usual wine-merchant to supply us with the wines which come, indubitably, from the classical areas.

Let us remember, while buying, that good wine cannot but be dear, and that, however dear, it recompenses only in part the care and experience of centuries that precede its birth.

Once in possession of the bottle, drink the wine respecting my advice and compare your judgement with mine. I have given it after many samples collected and examined throughout the course of the years. I want to stress that I have not come to a judgement of averages, but have confirmed as valid the one taken from the best samples, even if they were not the most numerous. This will allow the reader to demand, on the basis of my indications, wines which comply with the highest requirements of each type. The fact that it has been possible for me to find them in some samples proves the result which the care of cultivation and severity of wine-making can lead to.

One last note: I have not always given information on the ageing. I did not have first-hand experience of all the wines and I always wanted to rely on the opinion of my own palate and not on those of others. I will give you this information, completed, in the... 15th. edition.

We have walked along the Italian ways of wine.

I shall have succeeded in my task if my work is useful to the reader, who has given me his faith, and to the wine which I love.

Piemonte

Arriving from the surrounding regions, from the crowded Ligurian coast or from the asphalt jungle of Lombardy, Piedmont, with its ancient solitude full of silences, already gives the impression of a promised land, of an atmosphere and climate which seem to have been transferred from the green country of Umbria to the suggestive area of the Langhe, a sort of enchanted land in which Cesare Pavese lived and worked, creating a mosaic of personalities and unmistakable people who are now part of our literary patrimony.

It is useless to say that the great wines from Piedmont give one the same impression and make one aware of identical thoughts: it is enough to go a few miles to reach the famous places, Dogliani, La Morra, that hill rich in soft sandy stone, that part of the Langhe famous for its Nebbiolo, and one will immediately find oneself with a glass of strong wine which seems to open up true paradise. It is real Barolo, it is Dolcetto, which arouses inner feelings. Going further on, between Turin and Alba, between Bra and Asti, the ideas become more acute and sharper is the sensation of reaching an oasis of absolute bliss.

The greenish white colour of Cortese, the vivid straw colour of Castel Tagliolo, the muscat aroma of Brachetto and the pomegranate red and delicate, pleasing bouquet of Freisa are but small tastes of the mine which embraces the whole area and penetrates every angle of the vast plain to the slopes of the highest mountains.

Alessandria and Asti are in the centre of this sort of realm, small precious tenures in a farm of the greatest diversity: in Alessandria, Grignolino reigns, a wine which must be drunk young (after 4 years it is already too old) and which, with its vivid ruby red colour, its transparency and its perfume of woods, entangles one in its coils leaving no possibility of defence; nor is the Muscat of Asti less important, for delicate palates, with its intense aroma characteristic of musk and its frank, delicate and sparkling taste. Fill a glass and the white froth, light and persistent, fills your nostrils with the violence of a strong jet.

It certainly isn't fortuitous to find many Italian writers, whether they be from Piedmont or not, in the crowded inns of the land. Mario Soldati is at home here and it is enough to accompany him on a pilgrimage to know all these Temples of Bacchus, even the most hidden and isolated ones, perfumed farms on the slopes of the hill. Baldini, Cardarelli, Quasimodo, Montale also willingly allowed themselves to be guided by their friends who were born in the Langhe, by Beppe Fenoglio and by Cesare Pavese, in the happy search for Brachetto, Barbera, Barolo, Boca, and Freisa, for Agliè which takes one back to the world of Gozzano, for Chiaretto of Viverone, a delicious cherry-coloured, almond-flavoured wine, which is slightly sparkling but which goes at once to the head and makes one recite spontaneous verses as happened to our poets.

Piedmont is always able to give some surprises: a Carema, found by chance while going up the Val d'Aosta, a dry white wine of Asti, who knows how it escaped being drunk; a rich Barolo, which had become a warm chestnut colour, even veined like marble, and which came from the house of a host as secretive as he was a connoisseur; a black Barbera, a meal in itself, austere and powerful with tender roasts.

And there remains the oenological museum at Pessione to visit with tears in the eyes, because the instruments collected there, the amphoras and glass-cases filled with Greek, Roman and Etruscan vases, the urns of the guest Horatius, testify to a civilisation of wine which has now given way to fruit juices and orangeades.

Perhaps it was not by chance that the oenological museum found its place in Piedmont; for it is here that the archeological research of wine poses the greatest problems, those of mouth-watering and emotion. Here the enthusiast, always humiliated but tenacious in his almost scientific anxiety, is comparable to a mad pot-holer, in his complicated comings and goings in his search for caves and hidden rivers.

In this sad world the figure of an old Piedmontese gentle-man, whose memory goes back beyond the grave, takes on gigantic proportions.

He was an austere personality, naturally, even so he never ate "tagliatelle" which had not been capably kneaded by a special cook whose weight and shape gave to the delicate pasta an otherwise unattainable amalgamation. When he died, lying huge and hard on his big bed after two months of forced fasting, he asked for two things with his last breath: a piece of gorgonzola and a particular bottle of his own Barolo.

The gorgonzola was brought and he asked for it to be passed beneath his nose, his eyes closed. Then came the wine, a black bottle. It was opened and left uncorked beside his bed. After a minute or two the aroma began to invade the room. The old man dilated his nostrils, then lifted his hands.

"Bastards", he said to his relations, white and immobile around him, "this is not the Barolo from the third niche ...".

ALESSANDRIA

Cortese

Grapes of the Cortese variety.

Suitable for moderate ageing. Greenish white colour, delicate characteristic bouquet. Dry, with a pleasant almost imperceptible sharp taste, refreshing and light.

Alcohol by vol. 10-11%, total acidity 0.75-0.9%.

Superior table wine; if properly matured, suitable for hors d'oeuvres and fish.

To be served at 50 degree F.

Main places of production:

Acqui
Arquata Scrivia
Bubbio Canelli
Casalnoceto

Castelnuovo Belbo
Cessole Cortiglione
Incisa Scapaccino
Monastero Bormida
Montemarzino
Nizza Monferrato
Novi Ligure
Ricaldone
Rocchetta Tanaro
Serradio
Vesime

Barbera di Alessandria

Grapes of the Barbera variety.

Immediately ready for consumption, matured at 2 years, after 3 years loses its original tart taste. Ruby red colour, normally vivid, vinous aroma. Tasty, strong and genuine.

Alcohol by vol. 12-13%, total acidity very variable according to place of origin and year of production, from 0.7 to 1.2%.

Fine table wine, to be recommended with hot pork dishes and boiled meats.

To be served at 64 degrees F.

Main places of production:

Acqui
Altavilla Monferrato
Casale Monferrato
Cerrina
Mirabello Monferrato
Montaldo Bormida
Orsara Bormida
Ricaldone
Serralunga Di Crea
Villamiroglio

Brachetto di Alessandria

Grapes of the Brachetto variety.

Immediately ready for consumption, suitable for moderate ageing. Ruby red colour, characteristic aroma of roses; mellow taste with an almost Muscat flavour, generous, slightly sparkling; cherry red froth.

For some time a congenial dry Brachetto has been in production.

Alcohol by vol. 12-13%, total acidity 0.7%.

It is a wine which does not harmonise easily; to be recommended with some fruits (apples and pears) and for between meals. To be served at slightly below room temperature.

Main places of production:

> Acqui
> Cassine
> Alice Bel Colle
> Ricaldone
> Bistagno
> Strevi

Freisa di Alessandria

Grapes of Freisa variety.

Suitable for moderate ageing, garnet red colour, delicate and pleasant aroma.

Produced in two different types:

The first one with a slightly sweet touch, somewhat rough the first year, slightly stronger than the classical type of Chieri wine.

Fine table wine, to be served at room temperature.

The second is sweetish, of lower alcohol content, slightly sparkling.

Wine to be recommended with fruit, to be served at slightly below room temperature.

Alcohol by vol. 11-12% (for the dry type, lower for the sweetish one).

Total acidity 0.8-0.9%.

Main places of production:

> Acqui
> Bistagno
> Casale Monferrato
> Gamaleno
> Montechiaro d'Acqui
> Ricaldone

Grignolino di Alessandria

Grapes of Grignolino variety.

Suitable for moderate ageing (too old after four years).

Clear, vivid ruby red colour, very limpid; pleasing aroma. Dry, with pleasant, almost imperceptible bitter touch, delicate, agreeable.

Alcohol by vol. 11-12%, total acidity 0.7-0.9%.

Superior table wine; if properly aged, to be recommended with entrées and fowl. To be served at room temperature.

Main places of production:

> Alfiano Natta
> Castelletto Merli
> Odalengo Piccolo
> Rosignano Monferrato
> Vignale

VINO D'ORIGINE

LA MIA CANTINA

VESPAIOLO

• ACQUI •

VINO D'ORIGINE

LA MIA CANTINA

LAGARINO ROSATO

• ACQUI •

OR.FE.VI.
TORTORICI

OROVO
ITALIAN MARSALA WINE WITH ADDED NATURAL FLAVORING MATERIALS AND TRACES OF EGG

PRODUCED AND BOTTLED IN SICILY - ITALY BY

STABILIMENTO MAZARA DEL VALLO (MARSALA)
FEDERAZIONE ITALIANA CONSORZI AGRARI

NET CONT. 1 PT. 6 FL. OZ. - ALC. 18% BY VOL.

CINZANO

VERMOUTH

MEDAGLIE D'ORO MILANO 1881, BORDEAUX 1882.
UNICO PREMIATO CON DIPLOMA D'ONORE TORINO 1884

FRANCESCO CINZANO
E COMP.
PROVV.ri DELLE REALI CASE D'ITALIA E PORTOGALLO
TORINO

ESPOS. INDUST.

ESP. ITALIANA

VITTORIO EMANUELE II RE' D'ITALIA

LONDRA 1862
1862
LONDINI
HONORIS
CAUSA

FIRENZE 1861
ESPOSIZIONE ITALIANA DEL 1861 IN FIRENZE

DEPOSITATA

PRINTED IN ITALY

S. A. G.i DOYEN-MARCHISIO - Torino

LICENZA N.º 2

Casa fondata nel 1757

Moscato d'Asti

Grapes of the Muscat variety.

Dark straw colour; strong and pleasant characteristic aroma of musk. Fairly sweet flavour genuine, delicate, sparkling. Lasting fine white froth.

Average alcohol by vol. 7%, total acidity 0.5-0.6%.
Dessert wine. To be served chilled (57 degrees F.).

Produced in several districts of the provinces of Asti, Cuneo and Alessandria but particularly good at:

> Acqui
> Canelli
> Castagnole Lanze
> Castelletto Molina
> Castelnuovo
> Costigliole d'Asti
> Incisa Scapaccino
> Monastero Bormida
> Nizza Monferrato

A dry Muscat, aromatic and reasonably alcoholic, and a "Moscato Passito", amber in colour, with a good bouquet, alcoholic and of exquisite taste, are also produced in this area from the same kind of grapes by varying the method of wine-making.

Asti Spumante

Grapes of the Muscat variety with a small percentage of other varieties.

Its natural colour is amber, which is lightened for sale, bright; pleasant and characteristic aroma. Vivacious, white froth.

Average alcohol by vol. 6%, total acidity 0.6%.

Sparkling. To be served very cold, almost icy (39.2-42.8 degrees F.).

Produced in the same districts as the Muscat.

Barbera d'Asti

Grapes of the Barbera variety.

Suitable for ageing if of a good year. Pure darkish ruby red colour, which lessens with age, acquiring garnet red reflections; fresh and vivid vinous bouquet with a persistent aroma of morello cherries and sometimes of violets.

Dry, tasty, genuine and strong, becoming more delicate with age until it resembles certain characteristics of Barolo.

Alcohol by vol. 13-14%, total acidity 0.9-1.0%.

Superior table wine. Excellent with braised meats and tasty dishes of the local cuisine. To be served at room temperature.

Main places of production:

> Asti
> Azzano d'Asti
> Castagnole Monferrato
> Castel Boglione
> Castelletto Molina
> Castelnuovo Calcea
> Grazzano Badoglio
> Mombaldone
> Montechiaro d'Asti
> Nizza Monferrato
> San Martino Alfieri
> Villafranca d'Asti

Bonarda d'Asti

Grapes of the Bonarda (mostly) and Freisa varieties.

Suitable for moderate ageing, dark ruby red colour which lessens with age, acquiring brick red reflections; persistent sweet aroma of strawberries and violets. Sweetish taste

with a slight but noticeable touch of bitterness, sparkling. Alcohol by vol. 11%, total acidity 0.7-0.9%.
Good table wine.   To be served at slightly below room temperature.

Main places of production:

> Buttigliera d'Asti
> Castelnuovo Don Bosco
> Moncucco Torinese
> Passerano Marmorito

Brachetto d'Asti

Grapes of the Brachetto variety.
Immediately ready for consumption, suitable for moderate ageing.   Ruby red colour, characteristic aroma of roses; mellow, aromatic, almost muscat taste, full, pleasant, slightly sparkling. Cherry red froth.
Alcohol by vol. 11-13%, total acidity 0.6-0.8%.
If of an excellent year, dessert wine, normally not a table wine. To be served at slightly below room temperature. In recent years, a dry Brachetto of quite good quality has been produced.

Main places of production:

> Agliano
> Canelli
> Castagnole Lanze
> Castagnole Monferrato
> Montegrosso d'Asti
> Revigliasco d'Asti
> San Martino Alfieri
> Vigliano d'Asti

Grapes of the Freisa variety.

Suitable for ageing.

Garnet red colour, distinct strong aroma. Produced in two types:

One type is dry, at first somewhat rough rapidly becoming smooth, genuine and generous; more alcoholic than the classical type of Chieri wine. Good table wine; to be served at room temperature.

The other type is soft to the palate or sweetish, of lower alcohol percentage, sometimes sparkling. To be recommended with fruit, to be served at slightly below room temperature. Alcohol by vol. 11.5-13% (for the very dry type, lower for the sweetish type), total acidity 0.8-1.0%.

Main places of production:

Albugnano
Asti
Canelli
Castagnole Lanze
Castagnole Monferrato
Castelletto Molina
Castelnuovo Don Bosco
Cerreto d'Asti
Dusino San Michele
Grazzano Badoglio
Moncalvo
Moncucco Torinese
Montechiaro d'Asti
Refrancore
San Damiano d'Asti
San Marbano Oliveto
Tonco Monferrato
Vigliano d'Asti
Villafranca d'Asti

Grignolino d'Asti

Grapes of the Grignolino variety.

Suitable for moderate ageing (normally too old after four years). Beautiful, clear ruby red colour, bright; pleasing aroma of roses. Dry, with a pleasant, almost imperceptible bitter touch, light-bodied but fine, tasty, vivid and harmonious. Alcohol by vol. 11-12%, total acidity 0.7-0.9%.

Superior table wine, if properly aged, to be recommended with entrées and fowl.

To be served at room temperature.

Main places of production:

> Antignano
> Castagnole Monferrato
> Castello d'Annone
> Montaldo d'Asti
> Rocca d'Arazzo

CUNEO

Moscato di Cuneo

Grapes of the Muscat variety.

Straw colour, strong bouquet of grapes. Sweet taste, fresh, sparkling, somewhat less delicate than the classical Asti type. Lasting white froth.

Alcohol by vol. 6%, total acidity 0.5-0.6%.

Dessert wine. To be served cool (57 degrees F.).

Discreet sparkling wines are prepared from the same grapes but by a different process.

Main places of production:

> Castellinaldo
> Castiglione Tinella

Rocchetta Belbo
Santo Stefano Belbo
Trezzo Tinella

Barbera d'Alba

Grapes of the Barbera variety.

Suitable for ageing, provided it is of a good year and a good place of origin (e.g. Alba, Dogliani). Beautiful darkish ruby red colour; full vinous bouquet with persistent aroma, which in the municipalities of Barolo and Barbaresco, reminds the drinker of its most valued fellow wines.

Dry, genuine and strong taste.

Alcohol by vol. 13-14%, total acidity 0.9-1.0%.

Superior table wine. Excellent with braised meats and with special tasty local dishes. To be served at room temperature.

Main places of production:

> Alba
> Castagnito
> Dogliani
> Grinzane Cavour
> Monforte d'Alba
> Serralunga d'Alba

Barbaresco

Grapes of the Nebbiolo variety.

Matured and perfect at 3 years. Beautiful ruby red colour becoming garnet red with age, bright; delicate aroma of violets. Dry taste, less austere than the Barolo wine, soft, tart, of sustained and fine quality.

Alcohol by vol. 12-14%, total acidity 0.7-0.9%.

Exquisite wine for white-meat roasts and, if properly aged,

102

for red meat; blends exceptionally well with fowl. To be served at 6 degrees F.

Main places of production:

Barbaresco
Néive

Barolo

"Good Barolo ranks among the highest of the wine aristocracy, I would put it in first place above all the Piedmont wines were it not closely contested by Gattinara. They may treat each other like two good friends as neither is second to the other". (Paolo Mantegazza).

Grapes of the Nebbiolo variety.

Suitable for ageing. Matured after 4 years, perfect at 8. Noble ruby red colour, bright; this is lost after 6-7 years to take on yellowish orange reflections. Rich bouquet of violets, of tar and, more accentuated, of faded roses. Dry austere taste, velvety, full-bodied rich, harmonious, of sustained and fine quality, excellent.

Alcohol by vol. 13-15%, total acidity 0.7-0.8%.

Exquisite wine for large roasts of red meat and all game.

Open the bottles several hours before serving (In Piedmont, it is the custom to offer the guest of honour " 'n fund 'd buta", the bottom of the bottle uncorked the previous day). Should be drunk at 68 degrees F. in aristocratic glasses with rounded bowls of moderate volume and made of pure crystal, which brings out the qualities of the bouquet and the colour.

Main places of production:

Barolo
Castiglione Falletto
Monforte d'Alba
Serralunga d'Alba

103

Dolcetto delle Langhe e di Ovada

Grapes of the Dolcetto variety.

Ready for consumption after one year, matured at 2, rather old at 3, very old at 4. When coming from certain areas (e.g. Dogliani) or of certain years, can afford to have longer ageing. Clear ruby red colour if grown in sandy soil, garnet red if grown in chalky soil; subtle aroma. Notwithstanding its name, which is derived from the taste of the grapes, very dry with a very subtle sweetish touch, more generous but less refined than the Alexandrian type.

Alcohol by vol. 11-13%, total acidity 0.7-0.8%.

Superior table wine; very pleasant with sausages and salami from the high mountain areas (smoked beef, "mocetta" - smoked ham, and mountain ham).

To be served at room temperature.

Main places of production:

> Acqui
> Alba
> Barbaresco
> Barolo
> Casaleggio Boiro
> Castelletto d'Erro
> Diano d'Alba
> Garessio
> Mondovì
> Monforte d'Alba
> Montechiaro d'Acqui
> Ovada
> Rocca Grimalda
> Serralunga d'Alba
> Tagliolo Monferrato

Freisa delle Langhe

Grapes of the Freisa variety.

Produced in the same types and with the organoleptic characteristics of the Asti Freisa.

Main places of production:

> Barbaresco
> Castellinaldo
> Grinzane Cavour
> Magliano Alfieri
> Monforte d'Alba
> Serralunga d'Alba

Nebbiolo

Grapes of the Nebbiolo variety.

Matured after 3 years, perfect at 6. Beautiful dark ruby red colour.

It is produced in three types:

The first type is sparkling, pleasant, aromatic and light;

The second is delicately sweet, genuine and aromatic; and the last, the most valued, is somewhat rough at first, but later austere and aromatic and has some of the characteristics of Barolo, others of Barbaresco, but always less strong.

Alcohol by vol. 11-13% total acidity 0.7-0.9%.

The first, a sparkling wine, should be served rather cool; the second, a dessert wine, to be served at slightly below room temperature. The last, suitable with white-meat roasts and if properly matured, with red meat, should be served at room temperature.

Nebbiolo wines take the names of the localities where they are produced, thus they may be called Nebbiolo of Alba, Nebbiolo of Canale, etc...

Main places of production:

> Alba
> Cornegliano d'Alba
> Montaldo di Mondovì
> Santa Vittoria d'Alba
> Sommariva Perno

Ghemme

Mostly grapes of the Nebbiolo and Bonarda varieties, also Croattina and Vespolina from Novara.
Suitable for long ageing, matured after three years, perfect at seven.
Deep ruby red colour with amber reflections, bouquet of resin and violets.
Dry with a delicate bitter after-taste, velvety, tart, of sustained and fine quality.
Alcohol by vol. 11-13%, total acidity 0.8%.
Exquisite wine with white-meat roasts and if well aged, with red meat roasts and game. To be served at 64-68 F.

Main place of production:

> Ghemme

Similar types of wine are produced at Boca, Briona, Cavallino, Fara and Sizzano and take the name of the place where they are produced.

TORINO

Caluso Passito

Grapes of the Erbaluce variety.
Suitable for ageing, matured after 3 years, perfect at 6.

Golden yellow colour, exquisite typical flavour. Full-bodied wine, of warm taste, produced in two types: a sweet one and a drier one.

Alcohol by vol. 12-15%, total acidity 0.9%.

The sweet type is a superior dessert wine, to be served at 46 F.

The drier one is exceptional as an aperitif, to be served very cold, 41-42 F.

Main places of production:

> Azeglio
> Palazzo Canavese
> Settimo Rottaro

Carema

Grapes of the Nebbiolo variety.

Matured after 3 years, perfect at 5. Clear ruby red colour, bright; subtle raspberry aroma. Dry, with a pleasant, almost imperceptible bitter touch full and velvety quality.

Alcohol by vol. 12-13%, total acidity 0.8-0.9%.

Exquisite wine with entrées and, if properly aged, with white-meat roasts, to be served at 64 F.

Main places of production:

> Carema
> Normaglio

Freisa di Chieri

Grapes of the Freisa variety.

Suitable for ageing. Genuine garnet red colour, delicate and pleasing aroma.

It is produced in two types:

a dry wine, at first somewhat rough but rapidly becoming dry, austere, genuine, and harmonious. Superior table wine; if properly aged, suitable with roasts and fowl. To be served at room temperature.

The second one is sweetish or delicately sweet, of lower alcohol content. To be recommended with fruit; to be served at slightly below room temperature.

Alcohol by vol. 10-12% (for the dry type, lower for the sweetish one), total acidity 0.8-0.9%.

Main places of production:

> Rignano
> Chieri
> Moncalieri
> Moriondo Torinese
> Pecetto

Vermouth

Vermouth was first produced in 1757 in Turin.

Vermouth is a very famous special wine, obtained through the infusion of herbs and aromatic spices and produced through a long and meticolous technical process, in white wine of particular qualities. Its origin can be traced back to Hippocrates, the famous Greek physician of the fifth century B.C. (but the name seems to originate more recently from an Italian called Alessio, mentioned in history as an expert mixer of Hippocratic wines at Munich in Bavaria. Vermouth is a German word meaning absinthe and absinthe was used in the formula of that wine). Muscat wine of Canelli was used at first for the production of Vermouth; to-day white alcoholic wine from Sicily (Alcamo) and from Puglia (Locorotondo) are preferred. Vermouth is and should be nothing else but a good alcoholic white wine, flavoured with herbs. Its taste is usually bitter with a moderate sugar content; its class is recognisable by the perfect and well-balanced blending of its components.

It is the Italian aperitif; it is served neat or adjusted with soda water, strictly cold. Dry white Vermouth to be served at 39-41 F., sweet white Vermouth at 42-44 F. During the hot seasons, the adding of ice cubes is allowed. Both the classical and the dry types serve as bases for countless cocktails. Worth mentioning among the other types are the red Vermouth, which is served chilled; the Chinato Vermouth (with Peruvian bark added); and the bitter Vermouth.

VERCELLI

Gattinara Spanna

Grapes of the Nebbiolo variety.

Mature after 5 years, perfect in the following years until a ripe old age. Beautiful ruby red colour, bright, becoming, in the process of time, garnet red, brick red and bright clear orange.

Subtle and suave raspberry aroma at first, later a delicate bouquet in which roses and violets dominate. Fine and delicate taste, robust and strong; well-balanced, velvety, flawless; full, mellow, sustained and fine quality.

Alcohol by vol. 13%, total acidity 0.6-0.8%.

Aristocratic wine for roasts; also to be served with truffle dishes, red roasts and all game. To be uncorked a few hours before serving. To be served at 68 F. in elegant glasses with rounded bowls of moderate volume, made of pure crystal which brings out the qualities of both the colour and the bouquet.

A wine of slightly lower quality called Gattinara is produced with Nebbiolo, Bonarda and Vespolina varieties of grapes in the same area.

Mainly produced on the hillsides around the district of Gattinara.

Grapes of the Nebbiolo variety.

Mature after two years, improving with age, vigorous and excellent up to 25 years. From a beautiful garnet red colour it becomes slowly orange with age; delicate and penetrating bouquet of roses, violets and raspberries. Dry taste, sturdy, vigorous and genuine, smooth, harmonious quality.

Alcohol by vol. 12-14%, total acidity 0.6-0.8%.

Great wine with roasts and all game to be served at 64 degrees F.

Drink it with cold jellied quails (provided one has a good cook).

Main places of production:

> Lessona
> Mottalciata
> Valdengo
> Vigliano Biellese

In Mottalciata, Valdengo and Vigliano Biellese it quite rightly takes the names of Mottalciata, Valdengo and Vigliano.

Liguria

CINZANO

Asti Spumante

F.sco Cinzano & C.ia S.p.A.

TORINO

Giovanni Battista Ruopolo: Etalage de fruits de mer

The prudent visitor to Genoa knows that, in order not to suffer from the Summer heat and the Winter cold, he must turn into the maze of back streets and alleys which are protected from the sun and from the icy winds. He will then find himself in a modern City of Babel where, among the many languages which are heard, Italian is purely occasional and where, should he succeed in avoiding the inviting behaviour of some corpulent street-walker, he may enter either an ancient church or a no less hieratic wine-shop.

If the visitor would like something to drink, he must be careful not to say "mi dia un bicchier di vino" — give me a glass of wine; he must say it in any other language but definitely not in Italian. He would provoke who knows what reaction from the other customers because he would have qualified himself as "forestu", which means "intruder", unlike themselves who, coming from every corner of the world, are considered "at home" in that society. Therefore he must ask for a drink, perhaps even throwing a coin hard on the counter, by saying "un gotto!"

(a drop). Depending on the way in which it is said, the owner of the wine-shop, "u' sciù bacan", will understand that his visitor, even if he is Italian, is not altogether "forestu" and will serve him a drink with an effort of generosity and tolerance.

If "u' sciù bacan" scents that the visitor works more with his brain than with his arms, particularly in the naval industry or commerce, he will serve him, as is right, a "gotto" of clear, pale yellow, fresh Coronata, or of ruby red Canavese; if he thinks his visitor is an artist, a poet in particular, he will allow him to enjoy a wine of even better quality; but should he realise that his client is a withered Civil Servant or a professor from Rome, he will serve him without pity and with bad grace and malice the terrible "cancarone" (a horrible liquid) which has no mercy.

Another piece of advice: the wise visitor must not leave "u' sciù bacan" as soon as he has drunk his "little drop", or, worse still, leave his change as a tip; instead he must ask for another "gotto" and he will see that, for having appreciated the hospitality, "u' sciù bacan" himself will offer the third. Indeed it is even probable that he will offer it in "Italian", "n' atru biccer?".

At this point the visitor must begin to sing the praises of Genoa, to speak of this city as well as he can: he must talk about the great ship-yards, the industries, the blast-furnaces, about the great Genoa, "Genoa the Superb". He will show the flattered host how he appreciates the Coronata to the right degree simply because, in the complex of aromas which emanate from it, amongst which are sulphur and metal, there is a reminder of the active and industrial area of the Coronata wine.

The ice will now be completely broken and the enthusiastic host will offer (on payment!) the very best of his shop as a prize. Sciacchetrà levantino, perhaps with a touch of Schiacchetrau da Pornassio in it, which will loosen the visitor's tongue so well that even Italian will become acceptable.

And the owner of the wine-shop, "u' sciù bacan", will speak to him of the other various types of nectar produced in the area: he will talk with competent reverence of Cinque Terre, of Morasca Cinque Terre, of Limassina di Finale, and a hundred others ...

114

GENOVA

Coronata

Grapes of the Bosco, Vermentino, Bianchetta and Rollo varieties.

Pale straw colour, subtle bouquet; normally dry taste, fresh, very pleasant.

Alcohol by vol. 11-12%, total acidity 0.8%.

Superior table wine, also served with fish. To be served at 50 degrees F.

The area of production is in the district of the so-called "Grande Genova" (Great Genoa), mainly on the hillsides of Cornegliano Ligure.

Portofino

Grapes of the Bosco, Bianchetta and Rollo varieties.

White straw colour, delicate bouquet; normally dry taste, very pleasant.

Alcohol by vol. 11%, total acidity 0.7-0.8%.

Superiore wine with hors d'oeuvres and fish. To be served at 48 degrees F.

Main places of production located on the hillsides of Portofino and in some parts of the S. Margherita Ligure area.

Polcevera

Grapes of the Bosco, Bianchetta, Rollo and Vermentino varieties.

White straw colour, subtle bouquet, tasty, mellow to the palate, fresh, very pleasing.

Alcohol by vol. 11-12%, total acidity 0.75%.

Fine table wine also served with fish. To be served at 50 degrees F.

Main place of production:

Val Polcevera

Dolceacqua

Grapes of the Rossese variety (70%) and of the Dolcetto, Vermentino and Massarda varieties (30%).

Suitable for ageing. Ruby red colour, delicate strawberry aroma; tasty, light, with a touch of bitterness.

Alcohol by vol. 12-13%, total acidity 0.7%.

Superior table wine. If well matured, to be served with white-meat roasts and particularly rabbit. To be served at room temperature.

Bordighera
Dolceacqua
Isolabona
Ventimiglia

LA SPEZIA

Cinqueterre

Wine of great fame. Its praise has been sung by Boccaccio, by Sacchetti in the CLXXVII tale, and lastly by D'Annunzio in the "Feria d'Agosto":

"Fresche delizie avranno elli da scerre
bene accordate su la stoia monda
l'uva sugosa delle Cinque Terre
e nera e bionda;
l'uva coi suoi pampini e i suoi tralci
le pesche e i fichi su la chiara stoia,
e le ulive dolcissime di Calci'
in salamoia.

Infra l'ombrina e il dentice la triglia
grossa di scoglio veggon rosseggiare,
e il vino di Vernazza e di Corniglia
nelle inguistare..."

and again in the "Faville del Maglio":

"quel fiero schiacchetrà che si pigia nelle
cinque pampinose terre".

Matured after two years, perfect at 6. Yellow golden colour, slightly aromatic bouquet. Both a dry and a sweet type are produced, also known as Schiacchetrà and Rinforzato, and both have a warm but delicate taste.
Alcohol content varies a lot according to the year: 10-14% by vol.
The dry type is suitable with fish, the sweet one with fruit. To be served at 50 degrees F.

Main places of production:

Monterosso al Mare
Riomaggiore
Vernazza

Vermentino

Grapes of the Vermentino variety.
Suitable for ageing. Light straw colour, very pale, subtle bouquet; tasty, fresh, lively, harmonious.
Alcohol by vol. 11-12%.
Fine table wine also served with fish, but excellent with dishes dressed with "pesto", a Genovese sauce made of basil.
To be served at 50 degrees F.

Main places of production:

> Borgio Verezzi
> Castelvecchio di Rocca Barbena
> Finale Ligure
> Imperia
> Loano
> Pietra Ligure
> Ortovero
> Villanova d'Albenga

Lombardia

My introduction to wine goes back, very probably, to my childhood: at that time, wine ran freely in our house. We made it ourselves.

I admit it wasn't a great wine, but it was home-made and genuine. My father offered it to his friends with pride and satisfaction. The processes of production were long and fairly complicated and they occupied nearly the complete cycle of the year. They began with the pruning of the vines which amused us children as it was a good excuse to stay away from school. It is a pleasant job which requires light, almost feminine hands; it also needs taste in the arranging of the shoots and a sense of order, that they do not grow unbalanced when the leaves and bunches grow and ripen; that the rows match each other in a beautiful, compact, deep green.

The decision to begin the grape harvest did not usually depend on the ripeness of the grapes: my father and one of my brothers would come home from the fields one evening and say "Some children and gypsies have jumped across the ditch and plundered a row of vines; we had better harvest at once." So the next day we went into the fields, along the rows, carrying baskets, scissors and steps for the shoots which had grown up into the branches of the mulberry trees. We children also carried some bread in our pockets: the American grape is very good eaten with bread even if no-one believes me when I tell them.

We stayed out all day; at one o'clock we ate in the shade of the big trees and in the evening we returned on the carts which were black with grapes. On one small cart we put the white grapes, which were not many and which were always a bit acid; they pressed themselves and were used for making vinegar.

Meanwhile the "boat" — a big, long box of pale wood, impregnated with old must — had been put together in the cellar. For many years, there were officially only two pressers: one old and one young. But almost everyone got into the "boat", especially we children after having washed our feet very well in boiling water.

We jumped out bespattered with red like murderers; in the exciting atmosphere, made so by the fumes of the pressing, my brother poured us out some thick almost warm must in white bowls which coloured immediately. We dunked dry bread in it, unheeding the admonitions of the women that we would come out in a rash as, in fact, we nearly always did.

Then, when the wine had fermented and clarified in the barrels smelling of sulphur, it had to be blended with a stronger wine, which came from Piedmont or the South.

For many years, a man from Puglia owned a restaurant in the village. Lombardy had not yet been invaded by the Southerners as nowadays and therefore his presence among us was something unusual. In the Autumn, this man from Bari began to appear on our door-step and after a few visits he brought with him two or three little bottles full of strong, red wine. He went into my father's study and the blending operation began. Some years they did not agree, either on account of the alcohol content or the price. The Piedmontese entered the contest. Other wine-makers followed my father's example and consequently much court was paid to him.

With the coming of Winter, I remember, only one fat barrel remained from the harvest. It was swollen with dregs and it was enough to water it for a thin trickle of wine to run very willingly out of the spigot like coloured water. As the days went by, it became paler and paler. But certain labourers were content with even that: and so it lasted until the first snows.

Sometimes we used to go to Oltrepò, across the Po river, the great wine-producing area of Lombardy; three quarters of the wine drunk at Milanese tables comes from there.

Barbacarlo, bright red with a sweet taste; Sangue di Giuda (Blood of Judas), semi-sparkling and slightly bitter; Buttafuoco, which goes so well with game; Montenapoleone, with which to end a good meal: all these were still on the vines, next to the Riesling shoots, the Muscat of Scuropasso and the Pinot grape which came from France.

A friend (who accompanied us and who was a connoisseur and drank well with love and feeling) still reminds us of the Frecciarossa, with its deep aroma, so suitable with fish — and the San Colombano. This was the vineyard once upon a time: when the grape was cultivated even in the town, in gardens surrounded by high walls, and in the yards, with grass growing between the stones. A beautiful porch could not exist without a rich bower of vines to enhance it.

In the Valtellina area, the valley is narrow and cold but on the rugged slopes a few vines can be seen. The earth is tilled by hand, the land is stolen from the hill-sides. The wine from up there is called Inferno (Hell) and one can understand why. With Sassella and Grumello, it forms the Bacchanalian Trinity of the Valtellina. Their perfume becomes more refined with time as if it were worn by a beautiful woman.

We see the wines of Garda on the tables in the gardens at Lugana, by the side of the lake. Gathered on the banks between Desenzano and Peschiera, opaline, perfumed and dry, Lugana is perfect with fish.

The air of the lake transports us to Iseo where we find Franciacorta, bright red in colour, perfumed and rather dry. The little restaurant there used to be painted bright blue. But good wine was also sold along the road with wreaths of willows hanging from the branches. One drank for hours in the deep cellars.

In my father's library, I have found some old books which describe wine very nicely. On the first page of one of them is written: "Knowing wine is a secret for a happy life". It is Sunday, in the streets it is a feast day. The inns are full of people who, after having eaten well, are singing and drinking toasts. In the half-shadow of the room, I see the greenish light of a bottle of mineral water on a table. The voices and the songs fill the air. I wonder if it is not time, also for me, to reform: beginning, perhaps, with these so discreet wines of Lombardy.

BRESCIA

Valtenesi

This name is given to the wine produced in the area of the High Valtenesi.

Grapes of the Groppello variety (65%) with 35% of the Barbera, Berzamino, Corva, Nebbiolo, Sangiovese, Trebbiano and White Vernaccia varieties.

To be consumed the same year and, under no circumstances, after two years.

Ruby red colour, intense aroma; tasty, with a definite tart after-taste, fresh.

Alcohol by vol. 11-13%, total acidity 0.6-0.8%.

Table wine.   To be served at room temperature.

Main places of production:

Calvagese della Riviera

Monìga del Garda
Puegnago

PAVIA

Bianco secco dell'Oltrepò

Grapes of the White Croattina variety with other varieties.
Beautiful straw colour, bright; delicate aroma. Dry, fresh,
harmonious.
Alcohol by vol. 10-12%, total acidity 0.7%.
Fine table wine. Should be drunk at 53 degrees F.

Main places of production:

Casteggio
Pietra de' Giorgi

Clastidio Bianco

Grapes of Italic and Rhine Riesling varieties.
Clear straw colour with greenish reflections, characteristic
aroma.
Dry taste with a very pleasing sour touch which is harmless
to this blend.
Alcohol by vol. 12-13%, total acidity 0.7%.
Superior table wine with hors d'oeuvre and fish. To be served
at 48 degrees F.

Main place of production:

Casteggio

Clastidium Gran Riserva

Grapes of the Black and Grey Pinot varieties, which change
to white during the wine-making. Matured in Slavonic oak

barrels. Greenish straw colour, characteristic bouquet of roses and almonds.
Delicately sweet flavour, fine, harmonious.
Alcohol by vol. 12,5%, total acidity 0.6-0.7%.
Superior wine for fruit and dessert. To be served at 50 degrees F.

Main places of production:

Casteggio

Cortese dell'Oltrepò Pavese

Grapes of the Cortese variety.
Clear straw colour, strong bouquet; bitterish taste, definitely dry.
Alcohol by vol. 10-12%, total acidity 0.6-0.7%.
Fine table wine, also drunk with fish. To be served at 50 degrees F.

Main places of production:

Codevilla
Retorbido

Gran Moscato Fior d'Arancio

Grapes of the Muscat Orange Blossom variety.
Pale straw colour with gold reflections, very clear; pleasantly sweet with a definite very pleasant acidulous touch.
Low alcohol content, total acidity 0.6-0.7%.
Classical dessert wine (fruit and cakes). To be served cool.

Riesling dell'Oltrepò Pavese

Grapes of the Rhine and Italic Riesling varieties.
Pale straw colour with greenish reflections, strong aroma;

dry, harmonious, with a good body; after proper maturing, truly superior and exquisite.

Alcohol by vol. 12-13%, total acidity 0.6%.

Great wine with fish. To be served at a temperature of 48 F.

Main places of production:
> Casteggio
> Montaldo Pavese
> Mornico Losana
> Rocca de' Giorgi

Moscato di Casteggio

Grapes of the Muscat variety.

Pale strawish colour, strong characteristic bouquet. Delicately sweet taste, smooth.

Moderate alcohol content.

Main place of production:
> Casteggio

Gran Spumante dell'Oltrepò

Grapes of the Black Pinot variety, which become white during the wine-making, for which the "champenois" methods are used.

Aromatic and very pleasing; made in the following types: brut, dry, semi-dry.

Main place of production:
> Santa Maria della Versa

Barbacarlo

Grapes of the Barbera, Croattina, Uva Rara and Ughetta varieties.

Rembrandt: Le boeuf écorché

Suitably aged in small oak barrels, deep ruby red colour; delicately flavoured. Sweetish with a definite pleasant bitter after-taste (described in the district at similar to almonds). Lively froth.

Alcohol by vol. 11-13%, total acidity 0.7-0.8%.

Superior dinner wine. To be served at slightly below room temperature.

Main place of production:

Barbacarlo and Val Maga, in the municipality of Broni

Barbera dell'Oltrepò Pavese

Grapes of the Barbera variety.

Matured at 1 to 2 years. Bright ruby red colour but not as deep as that from Piedmont; strong characteristic aroma; tasty, slightly sweetish to the palate.

Alcohol by vol. 12-13%, total acidity 0.7-0.8%.

Table wine. To be served at slightly below room temperature.

Main places of production:

Bosnasco
Broni
Retorbido

Buttafuoco

Its name originates from a dialect expression "buta me-l-feug" meaning spatters like fire.

Varieties of grapes: Barbera 60%, Croattina 20%, Tinturino 10%, Ughetta and Uva Rara 10%.

Bright ruby red colour, strong characteristic aroma of violets. Dry, strong, abundant froth.

Alcohol by vol. 12%, total acidity 0.8%.

Fine table wine. To be served at room temperature.

Main places of production:

Broni
Stradella

Clastidio Rosato

Grapes of the Barbera, Croattina and Uva Rara varieties.
Pink colour, strong aroma; dry taste, slightly acidulous, fresh
and light.
Alcohol by vol. 11-12%, total acidity 0.7%.
Fine table wine. Recommended with soup. To be served
at 59 degrees F.

Main place of production:

Casteggio

Clastidio Rosso

Grapes of the Barbera, Croattina and Uva Rara varieties.
Ruby red colour which lightens with age to orange; deep
typical vinous flavour.
Dry taste, slightly tannic, full, harmonious.
Alcohol by vol. 11-12%, total acidity 0.6-0.7%.
Superior wine with white and red-meat roasts. To be served
at room temperature.

Main place of production:

Casteggio

Sangue di Giuda

Grapes of the Barbera, Croattina, Uva Rara, Ughetta and
Tinturino varieties.
Bright dark red colour, typical vinous aroma; almond taste,
mellow, characteristic froth.

Alcohol by vol. 10%, total acidity 0.7%.
Fine table wine. To be served at slightly below temperature.

Main places of production:

> Broni
> Montescano
> Stradella

Grumello

Grapes: 85% Chiavennasca (Nebbiolo), 15% Brugnola, Sassella and Pignola varieties.
Matured after 2 years, perfect at 5. Lively ruby red colour, bright; distinct vinous flavour (slight, almost imperceptible strawberry touch) which increases with age. Dry taste, with a slight sweetish touch, mellow, warm.
Alcohol by vol. 13%, total acidity 0.7-0.9%.
Superior wine with roasts; red-meat roasts and all game.
To be served at 64 degrees F.

Main places of production:

> Montagna in Valtellina
> Sondrio

Inferno

Grapes of the Chiavennasca (Nebbiolo) variety (85%) with 15% of the Brugnola, Sassella and Pignola varieties.
Matured after 2 years, perfect at 5. Deep ruby red colour, bright; lasting delicate aroma which increases with age. Dry, with a slight, almost imperceptible hazel-nut touch, mellow, warm.
Alcohol by vol. 12%, total acidity 0.7-1%.
Superior wine with roasts; red-meat roasts and all game.
To be served at 64 degrees F.

Main places of production:
> Montagna in Valtellina
> Poggiridenti
> Tresivio

Sassella

"I firmly believe that this is the best one can drink in the world. Many times has this experience been proved true: that the sick, forsaken by the physicians, believed dead and mourned by his beloved one, is revived by wine alone and given such life that his strength seems to be doubled". (Ortensio Lando).

Grapes: 85% Chiavennasca (Nebbiolo), with 15% Brugnola, Sassella and Pignola varieties.

Matured after 3 years, perfect at 8. Vivid ruby red colour, bright; lasting delicate aroma which increases with age. Dry taste, tart, warm, harmonious.

Alcohol by vol. 12-13%, total acidity 0.7-0.9%.

Great wine with roasts; roasts of red meat and all game. To be served at 54.4 degrees F.

Main place of production:
> Sondrio

SONDRIO

Valgella

Grapes: 80% Chiavennasca (Nebbiolo), with 20% Pignola, Brugnola and Rossola varieties.

To be consumed the same year and under no circumstances after two years. Clear ruby red colour, delicate aroma. Dry taste, fresh, quite harmonious.

Alcohol by vol. 10-11%, total acidity 0.8-1%.

Wine to be drunk with white-meat roasts. To be served at 64 degrees F.

Main place of production:
> Teglio

Trentino-Alto Adige

The Alps ... by this is meant the rough, high mountains; therefore those of Trentino-Alto Adige are Alps par excellence. *The idea of the Alps is linked with that of fresh, light waters, of springs, of splashing waters beneficial to the health. It may be supposed that wine, in mountainous places, in precipitous spots on the crest of the peaks, is not at home. But in the valleys, between one mountain range and another, in the poor fields, in the thin strips of land, next to the streams of clear water, among the great rocks where trout dart blue and silver, the grass grows exuberantly and takes on a deep green colour, on which the sun goes down even in the early hours of the afternoon.*

In these fields the hill slopes form ramparts to the higher spurs, the vineyards flourish and the short rows of small vines which form irregular perimeters produce tasty fruit, sometimes tart sometimes sweetish, but always full of character.

Sometimes the products of these grapes have aromas which recall ripe fruit — sometimes peaches, sometimes plums, sometimes

135

strawberries and black currants. The two provinces of Trentino-Alto Adige, Trento and Bolzano, are producers of many varieties of wine on account of the poverty of the cultivated land. White, red and rosé wines, suitable with certain typical local dishes, wines which mix the sweet fluency of early Autumns, perfumed like the Spring, with other wines made in zones with a harsh climate. In a word, wines from regions where there is sun, but where it lasts a short time and where the long season is that of the half seasons; therefore wines of composite characters, of mixed flavours. Also the colour of the Trentino-Alto Adige wines is a particular one: there are straw-coloured wines, wines which, when they are young, have greenish tones and when they are mature become golden with a faint flavour of almonds, with a full, round taste, but which reveal a quality of softness, suitable therefore to be drunk especially with fish.

Wines are like beautiful women, like great antiques, like the reflections of a precious stone, like, it must be repeated yet again, alive and beautiful products with their own character rather than their own characteristics.

Admirable things may be said of a wine and, if it were not known to what they referred, many things may be imagined. For example: "Mature after one year, perfect after three". "Beautiful clear garnet colour when young, verging on brick colour if mature, very clear, subtle bouquet, sui generis...". "Full taste, light after-taste of almonds, soft, slightly oily, harmonious". This refers to a description of the wine, Lago di Caldaro. Magic bunches of grapes produce this great superior wine, suitable with white-meat roasts, which should be served at room temperature; these bunches grow on the slopes of the hills which surround the village of S. Giuseppe on the lake and the region of the slopes of Mendola.

The experts, those who love the wines of this region, appreciate also Santa Maddalena, obtained from the Schiava and Schiavona grapes; it is a soft, velvety wine with an after-taste *which is rather pleasant to the palate, a full wine defined as superior with roasts, suitable for maturing.*

The variety of wines in Trentino-Alto Adige makes this zone a kind of miraculous oenological cove in the great massive body of the Alps, where even "elegant wines" like Terlano and Termeno — names taken from the places of production — are found together with Riesling.

Generally it is said "Bread for a day and wine for a year" but it is not always true, especially in the case of Teroldego, a wine which is mature after three years but perfect after six; also this wine smells like a bunch of flowers, tastes of violets, raspberries, almonds; its colour is violet-red, its aroma excellent, it is strong, full and round; it is a perfect table wine and with hors d'oeuvres. It is so appreciated that it is called "Princely wine of Trentino".

We have only touched on a few of the Trentino-Alto Adige wines but almost every valley in this region has its own and to list them all we must mention too many. It is therefore sufficient for us to deny the saying that where water is excellent, wine is less appreciated. In order to obtain a good product, we need excellent cultivation and this is had only when the quality of the product is appreciated: which is to say that this discussion is a closed circle. Good wine is produced when good wine is loved. And Trentino-Alto Adige is, among the Italian regions, one of those which, deservingly, aim at a respectable place in the oenological game.

BOLZANO

Sylvaner

Grapes of the Sylvaner variety.
Greenish yellow colour, typical taste of ripe peaches. Dry,
fresh, fine, vivacious.
Alcohol by vol. 11-12%, total acidity 0.7%.
Great wine with soups, eggs and fish. To be served at
46 degrees F.
It is produced in limited quantities in various places in the
provinces of Bolzano and Trento. Particularly appreciated at

Bressanone
Nalles

Terlano

Grapes of the White Terlander, Italic Riesling and White
Pinot varieties.

139

Outstanding for ageing. Clear vivid pale straw colour, with greenish reflections when young, golden when mature, bright; lasting delicate aroma.

Dry taste with slight sweetish touch, mellow, fresh, harmonious.

Alcohol by vol. 11-13%, total acidity 0.6%.

Wine to be drunk with soups and fish.

Main places of production:

> Andriano
> Nalles
> Terlano

Traminer Aromatico

Grapes of the Traminer Aromatico variety.

Dark straw colour, very individual aroma of vanilla, typical of the grape. Velvety, slightly bitterish, full-bodied, warm, strong, generous.

Alcohol by vol. 13-14%, total acidity 0.5%.

Wine suitable for fish soups and hors d'oeuvres based on sea food.

To be served at 53 degrees F.

Main places of production:

> Cortaccia
> Egna
> Termeno

Eppaner Justiner-Appiano

Grapes of the Red Vernaccia variety.

Garnet red colour, pronounced vinous aroma. Dry, with a pleasant, almost imperceptible bitter touch, full and agreeable.

Alcohol by vol. 10.5-11.5%, total acidity 0.4-0.6%.

Superior table wine. To be served at room temperature.

It is produced on the hillsides of the district of Appiano, mainly at S. Michele, San Paolo, and Missiano.

The type of wine which is produced at Missiano is also named Missianer.

Lago di Caldaro

Grapes of the Schiava, Grossa, Schiava Gentile and Schiava Grigia varieties.

Matured after 1 year, perfect at 3. Beautiful clear garnet red colour when young, tends to become brick red when aged; very clear, subtle bouquet "sui generis", typical of the Schiava variety of grapes.

Full-bodied taste with a slight after-taste of almonds; mellow, slightly oily, harmonious.

Alcohol by vol. 11-12%, total acidity 0.4-4.45%.

Superior wine with white-meat roasts.

To be served at room temperature.

Produced in the hills around Caldaro Lake.

Lagrein Lagarino Rosato di Gries

Grape of the Lagrein variety.

Pink colour, typical bouquet, with distinctive aroma of vanilla. Tasty, fresh, slightly sparkling.

Alcohol by vol. 11-12%, total acidity 0.4%.

Produced in the Valley of Gries (municipality of Bolzano)

Küchelberg - Meranese di Collina

Grapes of the Frankenthal (also called Schiavona) variety with other Schiava and Lagrein varieties.

Suitable for moderate ageing. Beautiful garnet red colour, pronounced aroma; dry, tasty, harmonious.

Alcohol by vol. 11-12%, total acidity 0.5%.
Fine table wine. To be served at room temperature.

Main places of production:

Lagundo
Lana
Marlengo
Merano
Sena
Tirolo

Caldaro

Grapes of the Frankenthal (also called Schiavona), Schiava Gentile and Schiava Grigia varieties.
Light garnet red colour, subtle bouquet "sui generis", typical of the Schiava varieties of grape. Dry, smooth, gentle but very pleasant to the palate.
Alcohol by vol. 11%, total acidity 0.5-0.55%.
Fine table wine. Blends very well with Speckknödel which is a sort of dumpling made from a mixture of flour and sausage. To be served at room temperature.

Main places of production:

Appiano
Caldaro
Nalles
Termeno

Santa Maddalena

Grapes of the Frankenthal (also called Schiavona), Schiava Grossa, Schiava Gentile, Schiava Grigia and Lagrein varieties.
Matured after one year, perfect at 2. Dark ruby red colour, tending to become orange with a subtle bitter after-taste, very pleasing, velvety, warm, harmonious.

Alcohol by vol. 12-13%, total acidity 0.4-0.45%.
Good wine with red-meat roasts. To be served at 64-68 degrees F.
Main places of production: Coste, San Pietro and Santa Maddalena, on the hillsides of the district of Bolzano.
A good white wine, Lacrime di Santa Maddalena, either dry or sweetish, is also produced in the same district: grapes of the White Pinot, Gray Pinot and other varieties.

Nosiola

Grapes of the Nosiola variety.
Suitable for moderate maturing. Yellow, golden colour, deep aroma; dry, very pleasant.
Fine table wine; if properly made, it is very good with soups, boiled fish dishes with mayonnaise and eggs.

Main place of production:

Lavis

Castelli Mezzocorona

Grapes of the Teroldego and Schiava (mostly), Lagrein, Merlot, and Grey Pinot varieties.
Ruby red colour, bright; deep pleasant aroma. Dry taste, full; right proportions of acidity and alcohol, harmonious.
Alcohol by vol. 12-12.5%, total acidity 0.5-0.55%.
Superior table wine. To be served at 64 degrees F.

Main place of production:

Mezzocorona

Marzemino of Isera

Grapes of the Marzemino variety (typical for its very small grape).

Deep garnet red colour, pronounced taste typical of vanilla. Tasty, sweetish, with a light tannic touch.

Alcohol by vol. 11-12%, total acidity 0.6%.

Fine table wine. Blends very well with "luganeghete", and local salamis made with garlic. To be served at room temperature.

A rosé type of this wine is also produced.

Main places of production:

Isera
Calliano
Nomi
Villa Lagarina
Volano

Merlot Trentino

Grapes of the Merlot variety.

Suitable for ageing. Beautiful ruby red colour with orange reflections, pronounced bouquet of strawberries and raspberries. Dry taste, aromatic, complete, harmonious.

Outstanding table wine. To be served at room temperature. It is produced in several districts of the Trentino region.

Casteller

Grapes of the Negrara variety.

Suitable for moderate ageing. Ruby red colour, aromatic. Tasty, strong, harmonious.

Alcohol by vol. 11%, total acidity 0.8%.

Fine table wine; excellent with "probusti", which are smoked pork and beef sausages, from Rovereto. To be served at room temperature.

Main places of production:

Calliano
Faedo

CASA FONDATA
NEL 1831

IMPORTATO
DALL'ITALIA

BOSCA

ASTI SPUMANTE

IMBOTTIGLIATO
IN ITALIA

Luigi Bosca & Figli
CANELLI (ASTI)
ITALIA

FERMENTAZIONE   NATURALE

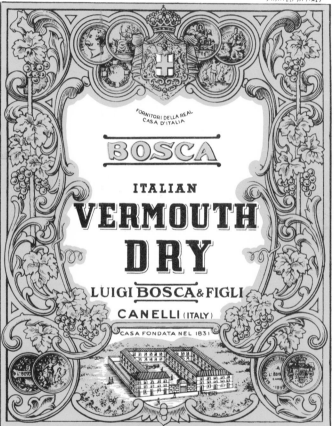

BOSCA

TRADE · MARK

LICENZA DI FABBRICAZIONE N. 103   *PRINTED IN ITALY*

FORNITORI DELLA REAL
CASA D'ITALIA

BOSCA

ITALIAN
VERMOUTH
DRY

LUIGI BOSCA & FIGLI

CANELLI (ITALY)

CASA FONDATA NEL 1831

PONZETTO - TORINO

Giovo
Lavis
Rovereto
San Michele all'Adige
Trento

Teroldego

Grapes of the Teroldego variety.
Suitable for ageing, matured after 3 years, perfect at 6.
Violet-red colour. Excellent compound aroma which recalls almonds, violet and raspberries. At first somewhat tannic and rough, gradually becoming drier until almost complete, full and strong. It is called "the leading wine of Trentino".
Alcohol by vol. 11-12%, total acidity 0.7%.
Superior table wine, especially for entrées; if well aged, to be drunk with white meat roasts. To be served at room temperature.
Its district is limited to the alluvial areas of the river Noce, called Campo Rotaliano, between Mezzolombardo, Mezzocorona and Grumo, which is part of San Michele.
A very appreciable rosé type of this wine is also produced.

Val d'Adige Etschalter

Grapes 75% Schiava and 25% Negrara varieties.
To be consumed the same year. Ruby red colour, normally clear; typical vinous aroma. Dry with distinct acidulous touch.
Alcohol by vol. 10%, total acidity 0.6%.
Table wine. To be served at room temperature.
Produced in the district of the Adige Valley.

Veneto

The experts define a celebrated wine which adorns the table as "a superior table wine"; it must be served with great care because it is a susceptible and precious wine which reveals its secret gifts only when the strict rules of its game are respected; therefore it is served only at room temperature and the bottles must lean, while the ruby red liquid is poured into a glass, at a rigorously controlled angle.

Such is Bardolino, as is also Valpolicella, which must be poured slowly, like a rosolio, because it effuses its typically vinous aroma with a distinct perfume of bitter almonds to the right degree. To the palate, Valpolicella is bitterish but pleasant, tasty and sparkling, mellow and fresh: it is a harmonious wine. This harmony is derived from the mixtures of grapes which are used in the making. The names of these grapes are enough in themselves to give the idea of the vigour and the flavour, and therefore to be convincing that Valpolicella is the result of a genial combination of various grapes: let us hear their names — Corvina, Negrara, which are the strongest grapes; Rondinella, Freisa, Lambrusco, which are used in a smaller proportion, are the grapes which give the flavour. From these comes Valpolicella, the wine which, rightly matured, may aspire to accompany dishes of white meat roasts: which is to say the highest aristocracy of wine. We have desired to put forward this detailed description of Valpolicella first as a stamp of Veronese wines; but what about Soave? The Latins, who were excellent drinkers, have bequeathed us wines and places of wine production, and very attractive descriptions in which they used terms and a style worthy of loving feelings, and also Soave is ennobled by this particular. Panvinio called its earth, the oppidum soavium, "vinorum optimorum ferax", fertile earth of excellent wines. Like the whole of Veneto, on the other hand, which is a sweet, winning region, truly suave in its sweeping landscape traced by the waving lines of the hills, the wines of this region maintain the characteristic of grace, unaltered even in the timbre of vigour which distinguishes it.

Soave, for example, is a clear, amber-coloured, light wine, with a velvety taste, having, however, one of the most definite and alert bodies within the Italian oenological panorama.

In about 1830 there was, so the story goes, a foreign lady who made the usual journey to Italy in order to complete her children's education. She travelled, as was then the custom, with her medicinal suitcase full of aromatic remedies against all illnesses: smelling salts, vinegar, lemons, aromatic herbs, brandy, etc. She felt ill on the road to Verona and the coachman, unaware of the precious chemist shop which the lady always carried with her, thought it well to make her drink a good glass of Soave in order to make her feel better. The lady opened her eyes as if by enchantment and asked for another glass of that excellent remedy. Needless to say, that miraculous new drink was quickly incorporated in the honours of her table and of her travelling chemist shop!

An exquisite wine is also Recioto which is produced after a scrupulous choice of dried Rece grapes, which are the best ones from the upper outside of the bunches. It is a noble wine, perfumed, rather sweet, mellow, a liqueur-like wine for the end of the meal, a wine which consumes itself in the mouth and gives a shock. A sparkling type is also produced.

The Veronese hills seem made to feed the vines and give good wine: they are hot and rich in humus, the sun filters through the tendrils of the vine at the right season and the water wets the plants when it is necessary in order to make the bunches of grapes swell, the climate of the region is suitable for the vine and appropriate for wine of quality. The panorama of the Veronese wines is completed by Bardolino, produced on the Eastern banks of Lake Garda, with the same grapes that are used for Valpolicella. It is a good table wine which should be drunk young, brilliant ruby red in colour, verging on cherry, with a fine and perfumed aroma, dry and full of vivacity and sprightliness, suitable with white meats and fowl.

Apart from the most famous wines, the region of Verona produces others in less quantity which are less well-known, but not less typical each one of its own particular qualities, like the red ones from the Veronese hills or from Valpantena, a ruby red in colour and having a "nice perfume".

In brief, this region which seems, at least according to local lore, a land of languor succeeds in giving us wines of great character which have imposed themselves on the world and which constitute a decoration for the most exigent and refined tables.

PADOVA

Bianco dei Colli Euganei

Grapes of the Garganega, Pinella, Serprina, White Pinot,
Prosecco, Italic Diesling, Rhine Riesling, Sauvignon and
Verdiso varieties.

Although suitable for ageing, it is preferred the same year of
vintage. Rather deep golden yellow colour, delicate aroma,
very pleasant; sincere, fine, fresh, subtle taste.

Alcohol by vol. 10-11%, total acidity 0.7%.

Fine table wine; appreciated with "zucca Baruca" (roast
pumpkin). To be served at 50 degrees F.

Main places of production:

> Arquà Petrarca
> Este
> Montegrotto Terme
> Torreglia

Moscato dei Colli Euganei

Grapes of the white Muscat variety.

Clear golden yellow colour, limpid, very pronounced typical flavour. Suitable sweet taste, very pleasant, light in alcohol and of good body, sometimes sparkling and frothy.

Alcohol by vol. 8%, total acidity 0.6%.

Dessert and fruit wine. To be served at 57 degrees F.

Main places of production:

> Arquà Petrarca
> Cinto Euganeo
> Teolo
> Vò

Friularo

The name of both the grapes and the wine is due to the place of origin. In fact, from Friuli the aristocratic Widmanns (wood traders, having established themselves in Venice from their native Carinthia in the XVIth. century and made Venetian patricians for services rendered to the Republic in 1646) brought the vines to their Bagnoli estate, from whence they spread widely in the provinces of Padua and Treviso.

The wine which was made from them met with such an enthusiastic reception that, some ten years later, a poet physician, Ludovico Pastò, praised it in a famous dithyramb, following in the footsteps of Redi, dedicated to Elisabetta Widmann Diedo; the poem ends with this refrain: "But of all the most appreciated wines, the best, the most perfect is this dear and sweet one, this blessed Friularo".

The Widmanns remained the exclusive producers of Friularo wine, in Bagnoli, until 1856, when they gave up the estate to Prince Peter of Aremberg, who increased the cultivation and improved the wine-making. The Friularo, wine which unites as many assets as defects, has not succeeded in conquering the markets, and its consumption is, in fact, limited to the province of Padua.

Grapes of Friularo variety.

Suitable for moderate ageing. Vivid garnet red colour which tends towards brick red with age, subtle aroma of morello cherries; austere to a point of harshness (due to an excess of acidity) and of moderate alcoholic content.

Alcohol by vol. 10-11%, total acidity 1.3%.

Table wine. Blends very well with small salamis "da gradela", which means "to be grilled".

To be consumed at slightly below room temperature.

Main places of production:

> Arre
> Bagnoli di Sopra
> Conselve
> Tribano

TREVISO

Bianco dei Colli di Conegliano

Grapes: 60% Verdiso, 25% Prosecco, 15% Malvasia Trevigliana, Italic Riesling, Bianchetta and other varieties.

Should be consumed the same year of vintage, because with age it loses its freshness becomes Maderized wine. Golden yellow colour with greenish reflections, very limpid; typical fresh and pronounced flavour. Dry with a definite bitter after taste; very pleasant, quite good body, a little tannic, fresh. Alcohol by vol. 10-11%, total acidity 0.6%.

Wine suitable with hors d'oeuvres and fish; particularly good with fried fish, which confirms the competence of Olindo Guerrini (Lorenzo Stecchetti), the author who wrote "The Art of Making Use of What is Left Over on the Table", who said in a poem "Fried sole and wine of Conegliano". He had learnt to like this wine, tasting it in the legendary Venetian Inn of San Pavan, which was also dear to Carducci. To be served at 50 degrees F.

Main places of production:

> Conegliano
> Pieve di Soligo
> San Pietro di Feletto
> Susegana

Bianco dei Colli di Valdobbiadene

Grapes: 60% Prosecco; 25% Verdiso; 10% Bianchetta; 5% Malvasia Trevigiana, Pevarese and Italic Riesling varieties.
It is produced in two types:
The first one, dry, ready to drink and to be consumed the same year of vintage, bitterish taste, smooth, light, harmonious. Good wine suitable with fish.
The second type sweetish, suitable for ageing, fresh, sparkling or frothy to be recommended with fruit.
Alcohol by vol. 11%, total acidity 0.55%.

Main places of production:

> Farra di Soligo
> Vidor
> Valdobbiadene

Cartizze

Grapes of the Prosecco, Verdiso an other local varieties.
Clear pale straw colour, delicate lasting aroma. Sweetish

taste, subtle fresh, light, harmonious. Natural sparkle.
Exceptional with fruit or as an after-dinner wine. To be served at 46 degrees F.
The production of a dry type of this wine, which is really first class, was started not long ago.

Main place of production:

Cartizze

Prosecco

Prosecco variety of grapes.
Golden yellow colour, sometimes deep gold, intense bouquet, of varying sweet taste, rather astringent.
Alcohol by vol. 11%, total acidity 0.55%.
To be consumed between meals. To be served at 46 degrees F. 46-50 degrees F.

Main place of production:

Conegliano

The wine-making from Prosecco grapes, either alone or together with Verdiso grapes, is very valuable for production of the so-called "Prosecco Spumante" (Sparkling Prosecco) which has gained merited and widespread fame.

Verdiso

Grapes of Verdiso variety (either alone or with small percentages of Prosecco and Bianchetto grapes).
To be consumed within a year. Depending on the method of wine-making adopted: golden yellow colour or greenish white, subtle bouquet, dry taste, astringent, fresh, delicate.
Alcohol by vol. 9.5-11%, total acidity 0.6-0.7%.
Very pleasing wine with fried fish, but truly exceptional with "risoto de bisato" (risotto with eels). To be served very cold 46-48 degrees F.

This wine is widely produced in the Marca Trevigiana region. The hillsides between Cappella Maggiore and Asolo are considered as the classical district for such a production. The types of wine made in Cison di Valmarino, Farra di Soligo, Pieve di Soligo, San Pietro di Faletto and Vittorio Veneto are particularly valuable.

VENEZIA

Tocai di Lison

Grapes of the Tocai variety (not to be confused with the grapes of the Hungarian Tokay, with which they have nothing in common).

Suitable for ageing. Pale straw colour, typical aroma, very pleasant.

Dry taste, with a somewhat bitter after-taste, velvety, less harmonious than the Tocai of Friuli.

Alcohol by vol. 11-12%, total acidity 0.6%.

Superior table wine (particularly suitable with soups and egg dishes).

To be served 46-50 degrees F.

Main place of production:

Portogruaro

VERONA

Recioto Bianco

Grapes of the Garganega and other white varieties.

Wine made from the dried "recie" (i.e. the best grapes which are on the upper and outer sides of the bunch) of white grapes.

Amber colour, full, noble bouquet. Mellow, soft and warm.

Alcohol by vol. 13-14%, total acidity 0.5%.
Liqueur wine for dessert.
To be served very cold.

Main places of production:

> Colognola ai Colli
> Monteforte d'Alpone

Roncà and in smaller quantities other districts of the area.

Soave

"Oppidum Soavium voluptate locique aeminitate sic dictum, vinorum optimorum ferax". Panvinio.

Grapes of the Garganega Comune and Garganega Grossa varieties (80%) together with 20% of the Trebbiano di Soave variety.
Suitable for moderate ageing.   Pale straw colour, clear; with greenish reflections when young, amberish when mature; perfectly limpid, typical bouquet with delicate nuances of vine, elder and cherry flowers.   Dry, tasty, with distinct flavour of almonds, velvety, fresh, gentle, thin but well-balanced.
Alcohol by vol. 10-12%, total acidity 0.6-0.65%.
Great wine with soups, hors d'oeuvres and egg and sea fish dishes.
To be served at 50 degrees F.

Main places of production:

> Montecchia di Crosara
> Monteforte d'Alpone
> Roncà
> Soave

Highly flavoured and of low acidity.
Alcohol by vol. 13-13.5%.

Bardolino

Grapes of the Corvina, Rossara, Negrara varieties together with Rondinella, Rossifinola, Barbera, Sangiovese, Nebbiolo, Freisa, Dolcetto Teroldego and Schiava varieties in smaller proportions.

Suitable for very moderate ageing. Ruby red colour, very clear; bright.

Vinous aroma. Dry, tasty, slightly but pleasantly bitter, smooth, light, likeable.

Alcohol by vol. 10-11%, total acidity 0.6%.

Superior table wine. To be served at room temperature.

Main places of production:

>Affi
>Bardolino
>Cavaion Veronese
>Costermano
>Garda
>Lazise

Valpolicella

Grapes of the Corvina, Rossara, Negrara varieties together with Rondinella, Freisa, Lambrusco and Barbera varieties in smaller proportions.

Suitable for very moderate agenig. Ruby red colour, bright; vinous aroma with a distinct scent of bitter almonds. Dry, with a pleasant, almost imperceptible somewhat bitter touch, tasty, sparkling, light fresh and harmonious.

Alcohol by vol. 11-12%, total acidity 0.7%.

Superior table wine. To be served at room temperature.

Another type is also made which, if properly matured, may be drunk with white meat roasts.

BOLLA

BREVETTO DELLA EX CASA REALE D'ITALIA

BARDOLINO

ITALIAN DRY RED WINE

HIGHEST AWARDS

PRODUCED AND BOTTLED IN

BARDOLINO - ITALY

BY

CASA VINICOLA FRATELLI BOLLA

VERONA

BREVETTO DELLA EX CASA REALE D'ITALIA

SOAVE BOLLA

ITALIAN LIGHT DRY WHITE WINE
SUPERIOR QUALITY

PRODUCED AND BOTTLED IN
SOAVE - ITALY
BY
CASA VINICOLA
FRATELLI BOLLA
VERONA
(ITALY)

BOLLA ®

NET CONTENTS
1 PINT 8 FL. OZS.

BREVETTO DELLA EX CASA REALE D'ITALIA

ALCOHOL 13%
BY VOLUME

VALPOLICELLA

ITALIAN DRY RED WINE
HIGHEST AWARDS

PRODUCED AND BOTTLED IN
PEDEMONTE - ITALY
BY
CASA VINICOLA FRATELLI BOLLA
VERONA

CORA

VINO

VERMOUTH CORA

CASA FONDATA — MARCA DI FABBRICA — NEL 1835

STABIL. VINICOLO IN COSTIGLIOLE D'ASTI

G. & L.

FRATELLI CORA

TORINO

1893 DEPOSITA

ALCOOL 16°5 – ZUCCH. 17%   CONTIENE 1 LITRO

CORA
LIC. N. 5
PRINTED IN ITALY
VERMOUTHS SINCE 1835
VERY
DRY
VERMOUTH
G. & L. FRATELLI CORA
TORINO
ITALIA
SPECIALE per COCKTAILS
PRODOTTO NEGLI STABILIMENTI DI
COSTIGLIOLE D'ASTI
S.A. Lit. DOYEN-MARCHISIO-Torino

Main places of production:

> Fumane
> Negrar
> San Pietro in Cariano
> Marano di Valpolicella
> Sant'Ambrogia di Valpolicella

Valpantena

Grapes of the Corvina, Rossara, and Negrara varieties together with Forcellina, Rondinella, Dindarella, Negrara, Barbera, Sangiovese and Freisa varieties in smaller quantities.

Suitable for moderate ageing. Clear ruby red colour, vinous aroma with very pleasing gentle bouquet. Dry, tasty, fresh, harmonious; if properly matured, soft and velvety. Alcohol by vol. 11.5-12.5%, total acidity 0.65-0.7%.

Superior table wine; if properly aged, suitable to be served with white meat roasts.

Main places of production:

> Valpantena
> Aninto
> Santa Maria in Stella

Rosso delle Colline Veronesi

Travelling East, one comes across the Squaranto, Mezzane, Illasi and Tramigna Valleys, where wines are produced with characteristics similar to Valpantena except for slight differences (less alcohol, more pronounced aroma).

According to the places of production, they take the names of: Valsquaranto, Valmezzane, Val Illasi and Valtramigna.

Main places of production:

> Cazzano
> Colognole

Mezzane di Sotto
San Martino Buon Albergo
Soave
Tregnano
Verona

Recioto

Grapes of the Corvina, Rossara, Negrara and other varieties. This wine is the result of a special process of wine-making in which only the "recie" (upper and outer grapes of the bunch), are used, which have obviously received the most sun. Deep red colour, full bouquet. Two types are made: one is capeble of complete maturing. The other is mellow and also dry, pleasantly bitter, velvety, strong, full, harmonious, capable of complete ageing. The other is mellow and also velvety, strong, full, harmonious, but only fit for moderate ageing.
Alcohol by vol. 12-13%, total acidity 0.75%.
The dry type is a great wine with game, the sweeter type for dessert.
The first one to be served at 68 degrees F., the second at room temperature.

VICENZA

Bianco dei Colli Berici

Grapes of the Garganega, Trebbiano, Sauvignon, White Pinot and Italic Riesling varieties.
Suitable for moderate ageing. Golden yellow colour, pronounced vinous aroma.
Sweetish to the palate, with a typical bitter after-taste of almonds, very pleasing.
Alcohol by vol. 10-12%, total acidity 0.8%.
Fine table wine. To be served cool.

Main places of production:

> Albettone
> Arcugnano
> Barbarano
> Brendola
> Castegnero
> Costozza
> Mossano
> Orgiano
> Villaga

According to the places of origin, it is also called Arcugnano Bianco, Barbarano Bianco, Brendola Bianco, Costozza Bianco, Orgiano Bianco.

Breganze Bianco

Grapes of the Garganega variety and also from other local varieties.

Pale straw colour with golden reflections, vinous aroma.

Dry, with an almost imperceptible but definite acidulous touch, fresh, pleasant.

Alcohol by vol. 11-12%, total acidity 0.95%.

Pleasant table wine, which blends very well with the most typical cf Venetian soups, "i risi e bisi". To be served at 50 degrees F.

Produced in the area between the Astico and Brenta rivers, mostly in the district of Breganze.

Garganega di Gambellara

Grapes of the Garganega (mostly), Torbiana and Trebbiano varieties.

Should be consumed within the year of vintage. Pale straw colour, with amber reflections; delicate bouquet. Dry and characteristic taste of almonds, which brings it close to Soave; fresh, subtle.

Alcohol by vol. 10-12%, total acidity 0.7%.

Table wine, particularly recommended with soups and egg dishes.

To be served chilled.

Main places of production:

> Gambellara
> Montebello Vicentino
> Montoro Vicentino
> Zermeghedo

Breganze Rosso

Grapes of the Marzemino, Negrara and other local varieties. Ruby red colour, full and pronounced aroma. Dry taste, moderate body, slightly tannic.

Alcohol by vol. 11-12%, total acidity 0.75-0.85%.

Fine table wine, superior with "torresani" which is a local dish of wild pigeon cooked on the spit with slices of bacon fat. To be served at 62-64 degrees F.

Main places of production:

> Bugane
> Lugo di Vicenza
> Maron Vicentino
> Zugliano

Rosso dei Colli Berici

Grapes of the Marzemino, Negrara, Cenerenta, Barbera, French Cabernet, and Black Pinot varieties.

Suitable for moderate ageing. Garnet red colour, pronounced vinous aroma. Sweetish and full taste.

Alcohol by vol. 11%, total acidity 0.8%.

Table wine; to be served at slightly below room temperature.

It is produced in the same area as the Bianco dei Colli Berici, but limited to the districts of Arcugnano, Brendola, Barbarano and Orgiano.

According to the places of origin, it is also named Arcugnano Rosso, Barbarano Rosso, Brendola Rosso, Orgiano Rosso.

At Brendola they make a special white wine, Ussolaro, which is rare and appreciated, but the grape from which it is made, the Ussolara, is slowly disappearing.

Friuli - Venezia Giulia

It has been proved that vines have been grown and wine has been made in Veneto since pre-historic times.

During the Venetian Republic, when the local nobility did not yet possess land on "terra ferma", wine was imported from Greece, Spain and Southern Italy.

Regarding the present-day production of the area, the wine of Friuli is to be especially remembered; that magnificent land, bordered by the Alpine range which runs from Gorizia to the Livenza river. The people of Friuli are tenacious and hard workers, accustomed to fighting against the invaders who have come in succession during the course of their history. They love the cultivation of the vine, which produces wine of good quality, and they pass this tradition on from generation to generation almost as if they find, in vine-growing, the courage to face all the adversities which are destined to come to pass every now and again.

On account of the two wars in the last fifty years, the people of Friuli have twice endured the destruction of their vine-yards, while they were fighting at the front or in the mountains during the partisan resistance of the last war. However, they have always reconstructed their patrimonial vine-yards, increasing and improving them.

It is surprising and admirable to observe with what love and expensive care the population dedicates itself to this cultivation, with the constant and traditional risk of losing it all again for the reasons already mentioned. It could be said that they gamble; however it is because they want to drink the wine of their own land, working it in the best possible way.

The ground cultivated as vine-yards in Friuli extends over about 250 thousand acres, and naturally the extent of the plains is greater than the hilly land, but it must always be remembered that the wine from the hills upholds the fame and is eminently worthy of the honour of the bottle.

Present-day production of the wine of Friuli reaches about thirty thousand tons per annum. Among the types of white wine, the following should be especially remembered: Tocai, Verduzzo, Romandolo and the famous Picolit, the production of which is unfortunately very limited, and therefore it is reserved only for the families who make it. Among the red wines to be remembered are Merlot and Cabernet.

It is sufficient to visit this land of vine-yards in Spring, to see the initial blossoming of the bunches of grapes after the first rays of warmth have touched them; the almost loving relationship between leaf and bunch gradually matures to grow joyously beneath the sun.

The Friulian farmer is very attentive: but Nature herself is so perfect that she compensates for that which Man may leave undone by her generosity. Nature has put everything in its right place; these vine yards run into the woods of chestnut trees which border the valleys at the top or along the sides and which absorb the moisture; the climatic conditions are the most appropriate there and the miracle of this harmony is manifested in the love of Man for this land, blessed by God, which he cultivates.

GORIZIA

Bianco del Collio

Grapes of the Tocai Friulano, Italic Riesing, Rhine Riesling, Sauvignon, Grey Pinot, Malvasia, Glera, Ribolla and other varieties.
To be consumed the same year of vintage. Vivid straw colour with greenish reflections, subtle bouquet; dry, tasty, with body, fresh.
Alcohol by vol. 11%, total acidity 0.6%.
Superior table wine with eggs and soups. To be served at 53 degrees F.

Main places of production:

        Piedimonte del Calvario
        Piuma
        San Flaviano del Collio

Picolit

I do not believe that in Italy there exists a nobler wine than this. It has been described as the automatic gem of the Friulana and Triveneta wine industry. It would be considered the pride of our industry if only it could succeed in establishing the cultivation and wine-making process. Unfortunately, first cryptogamic diseases and, more recently, a defect in its constitution, "the floral abortion" (which has been fought by a very famous oenologist, Mr. Dalmasso, by cross-breeding with other vines) have damaged it for a long time.

Without these misfortunes, to-day Picolit would have been the first among the Italian wines. In 1800, an intelligent vine-grower, Count Fabio Asquini, who owned Fagagna Castle, through particular care (for instance, he had the bottles specially blown at Murano) brought the production to such a point that he was able to export 100.000 bottles every year. It was the favourite wine at the Courts of Sardinia, England, France and Russia; the Emperor of Austria even declared it "better than any other wine". This opinion was confirmed at the Pope's Court at Castelgandolfo: "The other choice wines were left behind when compared with this one", wrote a priest to the producer, and in those days the cellar of Castelgandolfo was famous for its collection of exquisite wines. Unfortunately, to-day the Castle of Fagagna produces no more Picolit, and the vines have been destroyed by diseases. Giovanbattista Ridelli, exchanging the gift of six bottles sent to him by the owner with easy verses had an inauspicious prediction:

> Il vin famoso chiudere
> Medita in vetri puri
> Per così farlo vivere
> ne' secoli futuri.

Grapes of the Picolit variety, slightly dried.
Outstanding for ageing. Golden yellow colour; intense, full aroma, sweet taste, harmonious, sustained and special quality, very pleasant, unmistakable.
Alcohol by vol. 13-14%, total acidity 0.4%.
Stupendous dessert wine. I found it exceptional, very good with foie gras. To be drunk very cold.

Main places of production:

> Campeglio
> Manzano
> Savorgnano del Torre

Tocai del Friuli

Grapes of the Tocai variety (not to be confused with the grapes of the Hungarian Tokay, with which they have nothing in common).
Suitable for ageing. Yellow colour tending to lemon, delicate aroma slightly like flowers and almonds; mellow taste when mature, velvety, dry with a slight, bitter after-taste, full, harmonious.
Alcohol by vol. 11-12%, total acidity 0.6%.
Wine suitable with soup and egg dishes. To be served at 46-50 degrees F.

Main places of production:

> Colline di Buttrio
> Faedis

Verduzzo

Grapes of the Verduzzo variety.
Golden yellow colour, bright; distinct aroma of sweet almonds. Dry or sweetish taste, likeable, somewhat tannic, diuretic.
Alcohol by vol. 11%, total acidity 0.6%.
Superior table wine. To be served at 50 degrees F.

Main places of production:

Faedis
Manzano
Nimis
Tarcento

and in smaller quantities in other districts of this area.

Cabernet

Grapes of the French Cabernet variety with Cabernet Sauvignon grapes in various proportions.
Very suitable for ageing, mature after 3 years, perfect at 8.
Garnet red colour when young, becoming brick red with age, bright.
Full bouquet in which the scent of raspberries can be clearly detected.
Dry taste, tannic (while young somewhat rough, but becomes velvety with age) full, harmonious.
Alcohol by vol. 12-13%, total acidity 0.5%.
Great wine with roasts; both red and white meat roasts. If properly matured, recommended with all game. To be served at slightly above room temperature.
It is widely produced on the hillsides of Friuli; the type from Buttrio is particularly famous.

Merlot delle Venezie

Grapes of the Merlot variety.
Suitable for moderate ageing. Medium ruby red colour.
Pleasant, characteristic aroma. Dry, with an individual, almost imperceptible bitter touch, tasty, mellow, full.
Alcohol by vol. 12%, total acidity 0.6-0.7%.
Superior wine with roasts, particularly white meat roasts. It is widely produced on the hillsides of Friuli and of the "Tre Venezie".

174

Emilia - Romagna

SI BEVE FREDDO

ZUCCH. gr. 180   GRADI 16,5   CONT. c.c. 1000

LICENZA N. 7

PALAZZO CARPANO

TORINO   TORINO

TORINO

VERMUTH
DELLA FABBRICA
DI
GIUSEPPE B. CARPANO

1786

VERMUTH E LIQUORE CHINA   FABBRICA SPECIALE DI

LA PIÙ ANTICA FABBRICA DI VERMUTH

CASA FONDATA L'ANNO 1786 IN TORINO

CARPANO

Evaristo Baschenis: Natura Morta

There are seventy-two different qualities of wine in the provinces of Emilia and Romagna alone! Wonderful abundance and variety, and sad are these days when even the expert can find only three wines to describe in these districts: Lambrusco from Modena and Reggio Emilia, and Albana and Sangiovese from Romagna. Personally, I should add to these the white Trebbiano of ancient fame (which is not, however, as some write, the "Trebulanum" praised by Plinius). It is an honest sparkling wine which used to be sweeter than that produced to-day, in fact the poet Tassoni tells that Venus, Bacchus and Mars came down to earth to help the Modenese in their war against the Bolognese and their first evening in Modena "a una osteria si trassero in disparte ch'avea un trebbian di Dio dolce e rodente; - e con capponi e starne e quel buon vino - cenaron tutti e tre da paladino."

The Trebbiano of which the poet tells is made on the hills of Sassuolo; another type of Trebbiano is produced on the plains of Forlì which is dry straw colour and rather light. And

Cagnina (one of the rare feminine wines like Albana, Barbera, Freisa and Dôle from Vallese) which I drank at Terra del Sole, guest of the very learned Giovanni Giulianini, who praised that wine, while pouring it out, with Homeric adjectives, erythrós, eúphron, aíthops, vermiglion, joyful and vivacious; certainly I never saw a fuller or more scintillating red.

The "Gastronomic Guide", describing the wines of the region in detail, added almost another dozen to those already mentioned. Among the red wines Fogarina is mentioned, which is produced in the South of Emilia along the river Po, between Brescella and Gualtieri — not very strong, a very pale violet colour, with a red froth and an aroma of raspberries and blackcurrants. (It can't be very good - Mazzacurati, the sculptor, who come from Gualtieri, has never mentioned it to me!). The black wine from Bosco Eliseo near Comacchio is also mentioned which is drunk in great quantities with eels, together with the mellow red wines and sparkling wines from Piacenza. The list of white wines, which the people from Emilia and Romagna value more, is richer: Aleatico from Bertinoro and that from Modigliana, Malvasia from Maiatico and that from Roccalanzona; the "vin santo" from Ponte dell'Olio and from Soragna; and a very alcoholic tocai from Gropparello in the province of Piacenza.

Naturally, Emilia and Romagna being one among the four or five greatest producing regions in Italy, one finds there a great quantity of unknown wines; and it is best to drink them where they are found, accompanied by local cooking which is heavy and tasty and strong and is served in large portions and needs ordinary wines, without too much fuss and maturity. Indeed, Albana, Lambrusco and Sangiovese are never asked for outside their own district unless by some exiled person from those parts; they are tasty, exhilarating drinks but they do not go very well with refined food. Lambrusco from Sorbara is never so good as when drunk with "zampone" which is a delicious dish but very rustic, or with "crescenta", a farm bread obtained by kneading water and flour with some lard and salt, and nothing more; the beaten lump, flattened by the palm of the hand, is slid into a pan where lard and oil have been heated, and fried over a wood fire. Lambrusco from the hills goes especially well with green "lasagna" (a Bolognese specialty of pasta baked in the oven) and with rice balls, or better still with "calzagatti", that is fried polenta with boiled beans. Albana, which is slightly sweet and loosens the tongue, is the right company for the pork, mortadella and salami of Romagna; and Sangiovese, sturdy and strong, is the natural liquid tomb for "cappelletti" which are a larger form af "tortellini" than those of Bologna, and with a plate full of curds, eggs, pork, chicken, pepper and nuts which is not for a delicate stomach!

In short, they are provincial wines: one would not dare to adorn the table of a king or a bishop with them: not one of these heavy drinkers who get drunk regularly once a month or once a fortnight to keep in good health would want to do so on one of these little-alcoholic wines (Lambrusco contains very little alcohol and Albana is perfumed like a young bride).

I must say that Lambrusco, among the provincial wines, is the noblest. It was already so in Roman times and, with the centuries, the vine has been domesticated. It does not like to get old: after two or three years it is at its best and has acquired a perfume of violets which is its distinction.

Sangiovese is also a wine for passionate people. It is stronger than Lambrusco but has a certain gentility which vaguely reminds one of Chianti.

A wine from Romagna which enjoys greater fame than it really deserves is Albana, for its beautiful name, I think, which conjures up adventure and remoteness.

BOLOGNA

Albana di Romagna

"A traveller ordered a bottle of Albana wine, but he wanted
it from Bertinoro. 'The Albana is from nowhere else but
Bertinoro', said the waiter, shrugging his shoulders". (Ric-
cardo Bacchelli).

Grapes of the Albana variety.

Wine suitable for moderate ageing. Golden yellow colour
with amberish reflections; exquisite and unmistakable flavour.

Dry taste, or suavely sweetish to the palate, soft, full-bodied,
sustained and generous quality, harmonious, very pleasant.
Alcohol by vol. 12-12.5%, total acidity 0.5-0.6%.

Superior table wine, exceptional with fish soup and snails.
To be served at 53 degrees F.

A sweet dessert type is also produced.

Main places of production:

> Bertinoro
> Castrocaro e Terra del Sole
> Cesena
> Dovadola
> Forte
> Forlimpopoli
> Mèldola
> Rimini
> Savignano sul Rubicone

Sangiovese

Grapes of the Sangiovese variety.
Suitable for ageing.   Rather deep vivid ruby red colour, pleasant aroma which changes, with age, to a bouquet. Dry taste, sometimes a little tannic, with a very pleasing slightly bitter after-taste; neither too light nor too heavy.
Alcohol by vol. 11-13%, total acidity 0.5-0.7%.
Superior table wine and, if properly aged, suitable with red meat roasts.
To be served at room temperature.
It is produced in a very large area, particularly at:

> Castrocaro e Terra del Sole
> Cesena
> Forlì
> Mèldola
> Predappio
> Rimini

MODENA

Lambrusco Graspa Rossa

"It is somewhat heavy for delicate stomachs, but it is preferred by the tradesmen from North of the Po who, thanks to its

182

deep colour and high alcohol content, revive the miracle of the Last Supper while the bottles are crossing the river Po". (Agazzotti).

It has organoleptic characteristics rather similar to those of Lambrusco of Sorbara, but it has less consistency and a deeper colour.

Main places of production:

> Castelfranco Emilia
> Castelvetro di Modena
> Fiorano Modenese
> Modena
> Sassuolo
> Spilamberto
> Vignola

Lambrusco di Sorbara

The Lambrusco of Sorbara has a special quality: it is 'human'. No other wine in the world recalls so vividly the idea of patriarchy and daily life.

Grapes of the Lambrusco variety (mostly) with other local varieties.

Suitable for very moderate ageing. Beautiful ruby red colour, bright; distinct, deep violet aroma. Dry, tasty, fresh, very likeable. Vivid red froth.

Alcohol by vol. 11%, total acidity 0.9-1.1%.

Very pleasing table wine, which is outstanding with some local dishes, such as "zampone" with lentils and home-made pasta known as "cappelli da prete" (priests' hats) on account of their shape. It is exquisite with river trout prepared with butter and sage although these qualities are not sufficiently known.

To be served at slightly below room temperature (60 F.).

Main places of production:

> Carpi
> Modena
> Ravanino
> Sorbara
> San Prospero

Barbera di Langhirano

Grapes of the Barbera variety.
Suitable for moderate ageing. Deep red colour, weak vinous aroma. Dry taste, sincere, full, strong.
Alcohol by vol. 11%, total acidity 0.8-0.9%.
Fine table wine. It blends very well with properly seasoned Felino salami.
To be served at room temperature.

Main places of production:

> Fidenza
> Fornovo di Taro
> Medesano
> Salsomaggiore
> Traversetolo

PIACENZA

Monterosso

"Castello Arquato produces excellent wines and it is a great shame that the hill is not entirely covered by vineyards from which come wines as delicate as those which can be found in the whole of Lombardy ... both white and red.
It is here that His Holiness made provision for His journey and where He sent for it even when he was in Ferrara or Bologna". Sante Lancerio.

Grapes of the Santamaria, Belverdino and Trebbiano varieties.
To be consumed within the year of vintage. Pale straw colour,
very limpid, delicate aroma.
Dry taste, with a distinct sweetish touch, light, sparkling.
Alcohol by vol. 10-11%, total acidity 0.7%.
Table wine to be served at 53 degrees F.

Main places of production:

> Castell'Arquato
> Lugagnano Val d'Arda
> Vernasca

Trebbiano

Grapes of the Trebbiano, Ortugo and Malvasia varieties.
To be consumed within the year. Pale straw colour, typical
"sui generis" aroma, which reminds one of saffron. Moderately
sweet taste; sincere, sparkling.
Alcohol by vol. 9-11%, total acidity 0.6%.
Good wine for fruit or to be consumed between meals. To
be served at 53 degrees F.
Produced in the Valley of the Trebbia river, particularly at:

> Bobbio
> Riverzano
> Vigolzone

A dry and sincere type of wine, which blends very well with
trout from the Trebbia river and with local snails, it is
produced at Bobbio from the Trebbiano variety of grapes only.

Gutturnio

Grapes of the Barbera (70%) and Bonarda (30%) varieties.
To be consumed within the year. Garnet red colour, vinous
aroma. Dry, with a light sweetish touch and an almost
imperceptible bitter taste like almonds, full, pleasing.

Alcohol by vol. 11%, total acidity 0.7%.
Table wine. To be served at slightly below room temperature (60 degrees F.).

Main places of production:

> Carpaneto Vicentino
> Castel San Giovanni
> Ponte dell'Olio
> Ziano Vicentino

REGGIO EMILIA

Scandiano

Grapes of local white varieties.
Pale straw colour with greenish reflections. Likeable taste.
Dry, with a slightly acidulous touch, fresh, very pleasing.
Alcohol by vol. 10%, total acidity 0.6%.
Fine table wine suitable with fish (especially with small trout).
To be served at 53 degrees F.

Main places of production:

> Albinea
> Scandiano

A sweet sparkling wine is also produced.

Lambrusco Salamino

Grapes of the Lambrusco Salamino variety.
Suitable for moderate ageing. Beautiful, rather deep, ruby red colour; full, vinous aroma. Dry taste, sincere, subtly

astringent, sparkling or frothy. Not very lasting red froth.
Alcohol by vol. 11%, total acidity 0.85%.
Likeable table wine. To be served at slightly below room
temperature (60 degrees F.).

Main places of production:

   Campagnolo Emilia
   Correggio
   Rio Saliceto
   Rubina
   San Martino in Rio

Toscana

Tuscan wine, and in particular Chianti, is so characteristic, so famous that already for many centuries it has been one of the symbols of oleographic and post card Italy, as are the pizza, spaghetti, mandolins and the plumes of the Bersaglieri.

Best of all the Grand Duchy wines is naturally the Chianti. The young Chianti is ruby red colour, vivacious but not intense with a particular vinous aroma and has a pleasing taste: fresh and as every classic wine it is even sparkling in its adolescence.

Generally it can be drunk after 6 months of processing in the cellar. When it is of noble origin it must be kept two or even three years before reaching full maturity. The ruby red of the noble Chianti has some yellowish reflections, an intense, characteristic and very pleasant aroma, and a dry, harmonious and velvety taste.

One uses a less proud pen to describe Tuscany's white wines. However, Pomino from Val di Sieve and Montecarlo from Lucca go very well with fish and the white wines, which are slightly green in colour, tasty and a little acid, and which are made from the

191

Trebbiana grape, are not at all unpleasant. White Procanico from Elba is very chic; and Aleatico and Muscat are really special. Vinsanto, really worthy of the Medici family, is a wine into which certain Florentine biscuits, made of almonds, flour and honey, may be dunked.

The nobility of Tuscan wine is affirmed in poetry. Chianti, Carmignano and Montepulciano have all been praised by the poets, and not by minor ones. Among these is Francesco Redi who proclaimed the noble wine as "the King of all wines". He wrote a poem, a dithyramb, called "Bacchus in Tuscany":

> In quel vetro che chiamasi il tonfano
> scherzan le Grazie e vi trionfano;
> ognun colmilo, ognun vuotilo:
> ma di che si colmerà?
> Bella Arianna, con bianca mano
> versa la manna di Montepulciano;
> colmane il tonfano e porgilo a me.
> Questo liquore che sdrucciola al core,
> oh come l'ugola baciami e mordemi!
> oh come in lacrime gli occhi disciogliemi!
> Me ne strassecolo, me ne strabilio,
> e fatto estatico vo in visibilio.
> Onde ognun che di Lieo
> riverente il nome adora
> ascolti questo altissimo decreto,
> che Bassareo pronunzia, e gli dia fé:
> Montepulciano d'ogni vino è il re!

The Tuscans boast that their wine has at least five centuries of nobility behind it. We can easily believe them if we read "I Beoni" by Lorenzo de' Medici, the peasant poem, dedicated to his drunken friends. It was Autumn, the season of Bacchus, when the young poet met his friend Bartolino outside the gate of Faenza. Where are you going in such a hurry, oh Bartolino?

> Quel che tu vuoi convien che alfin ti dica,
> benché l'andar sia in fretta, come vedi,
> per la cagion che appresso a te si esplica.
> Tutti ne andiam verso il Ponte a Rifredi
> che Giannesse ha spillato un botticello
> di vin che presti facci i lenti piedi.
> Tutti n'andiamo in fretta a ber con quello,
> quel ci fa sol sì presti in sulla strada,
> e veloce ciascun più che un uccello.

192

Brolio Riserva

CHIANTI CLASSICO

CASA VINICOLA
BARONE RICASOLI
FIRENZE

IMBOTTIGLIATO AL CASTELLO DI BROLIO IN CHIANTI

PRINTED IN ITALY   ANGIOLINI & VISIBELLI - LUCCA

CONTENT 1 PINT 8 FL. OZ. ACOHOL 13% BY VOL. PRODUCE OF ITALY
IMPORTED BY **BROWNE VINTNERS CO., INC.,** NEW YORK, N. Y.
SOLE DISTRIBUTORS FOR THE U.S.A.

Even the haughty French of the Roi Soleil deigned, with great condescension, to concede that "Tuscan wine" has some merits. The "Nouveau Voyage d'Italie, avec un Memoire contenant des avis utiles à ceux qui voudront faire la même voyage", edited by Henry Van Bulderen in the Hague in 1702 says: "A Florence et à Montefiascone les meilleurs vins sont agréables; et n'ont pas plus de feu qu'il n'en faut, pour la boisson ordinaire; mais il n'y en a qu'en petite quantité. Le délicat Moscadello du Gran Duc est un petit vignoble sacré pour sa bouche, ou pour des présents. Il ne faut pas s'imaginer que cette liqueur soit répandu par tout le pays."

Besides, Vernaccia has been famous since Dante's time, or rather we should say since Cecco degli Angiolieri who was undoubtedly the prince and poet of the drinkers. In "Ditirambo" by Redi, Bacchus shouts and threatens thus:

> Se v'è ancuno a cui non piaccia
> la Vernaccia
> vendemmiata in Pietrafitta,
> interdetto, maledetto
> fugga via dal mio cospetto
> . . . .
> e per onta e per ischerno
> in eterno
> coronato sia di bietola.

Finally the glory of Chianti is affirmed even in the streets of New York: on the backs of the buses there are large red advertisements for a brand of Chianti. Extremely efficient publicity: whoever moves about in New York has the name of Chianti continuously in front of his eyes.

AREZZO

Chianti dei Colli Aretini

Grapes of the Sangioveto variety with Trebbiano, Malvasia, and Canaiolo varieties.

Suitable for moderate ageing. Ruby red colour, which tends to garnet red with age, very aromatic. Dry taste sincere, fresh, sparkling at times, harmonious.

Alcohol by vol. 11.5-12.5%, total acidity 0.6-0.7%.

Superior table wine. To be served at room temperature.

It is produced in a large area, particularly:

> Arezzo
> Civitella in Val di Chiana
> Pergine
> Montegonzi

Valchiana

This wine is also called *Vergine della Val di Chiana* (Virgin of the Chiana Valley) because it is made with the fruit only of the bunch, and it is taken off the stems with the greatest of care.

Grapes of the Trebbiano and other local varieties.

Greenish white colour, very limpid; delicate aroma. Dry taste with a distinct acidulous touch, very pleasant, tasty, fresh. Alcohol by vol. 11-12%, total acidity 0.6-0.7%.

Fine table wine suitable with fish. To be served at 46 degrees F.

Main places of production:

> Arezzo
> Castiglione Fiorentino
> Civitella in Val di Chiana
> Cortona
> Monte San Savino

Carmignano

Grapes of the Sangioveto (mostly), Canaiolo, Trebbiano, Malvasia and Colorino varieties.

Suitable for ageing. Vivid ruby red colour, bright; deep aroma of sweet violets.

Dry taste, velvety, less fine than the classical Chianti, but, in compensation, more complete, fuller and tastier.

Alcohol by vol. 12-13%, total acidity 0.6-0.8%.

Superior table wine and, if properly matured, suitable with red and white-meat roasts and all game. To be served at 64-68 degrees F.

Main place of production:

> Carmignano

An appreciatable white wine is also produced in this district with organoleptic characteristics similar to White Capezzana, also called Carmigiano Bianco.

In the district of Artimino, a wine which takes its name from the area and which has organoleptic characteristics identical to those of Carmignano is made too.

FIRENZE

Chianti Rufina

Grapes of the Sangioveto variety (60%) with Trebbiano, Malvasia and Caniolo, varieties.

Suitable for ageing. When young, it is a very dark ruby red colour, which improves with age to a brilliant ruby red colour; definite aroma of fruit.

Dry taste, with subtle sweetish touch, tasty, smooth, well-balanced.

Alcohol by vol. 11-13%, total acidity 0.6-0.7%.

Superior table wine and, if properly aged, suitable with roasts. To be served at 64 degrees F.

Main place of production:

> Rufina
> Dicomano
> Doccia
> Nipozzano
> Pontassieve

Chianti dei Colli Fiorentini

Grapes of the Sangioveto, Canaiolo, Trebbiano, Malvasia.

Ruby red colour, bright; very aromatic. Dry taste, fresh, pleasant, harmonious.

Alcohol by vol. 11.5-12.5%, total acidity. 0.7%.

Superior table wines. To be served at 64 degrees F.

Main places of production:

> Bagni a Ripoli
> Barberino Val d'Elsa
> Fiesole
> Tavernelle Val di Pesa

GROSSETO

Ansonica

Grapes of the Ansonica, Spagna Bianca and Biancone varieties.
Suitable for moderate maturing. Pale straw colour with amber
reflections; subtle aroma. Dry, tasty, fresh, generous.
Alcohol by vol. 12-15%, total acidity 0.7%.
Superior table wine suitable with fish. Outstanding with
shell-fish.
To be served at 46 degrees F. A sweetish type for dessert
is also produced.

Main places of production:

> Isola del Giglio
> Monte Argentario

LIVORNO

Moscato dell'Elba

Grapes of the Muscat variety.
Golden yellow colour, bright; deep typical aroma. Sweet
taste, generous, alcoholic, rich in phosfo-ferro-arsenious
compounds.
Alcohol by vol. 14-15%, total acidity 0.6%.

Great dessert wine and for between meals.

Produced in the Island of Elba.

Appreciatable natural sparkling wines are made in the Island of Elba from the Muscat variety of grapes.

Aleatico di Portoferraio

Grapes of the Aleatico variety.

Suitable for ageing. Very deep ruby red colour. (Ugo Ojetti wrote: "The trays laden with tinkling glasses and flasks of Aleatico of a dark purple colour were brought in".) Penetrating bouquet; sweet taste, exquisite, mellow, generous, rich in phosfo-ferro-arsenious compounds.

Alcohol by vol. 12-15%, total acidity 0.6-0.7%.

Great dessert wine.

To be served at 57 degrees F.

Produced in the Island of Elba.

LUCCA

Montecarlo Bianco

Grapes of the Trebbiano (mostly) and other local varieties. Suitable for moderate ageing. Pale straw colour, clear and bright; subtle aroma. Dry, tasty, velvety, light, well-balanced. Alcohol by vol. 13%, total acidity 0.7%.

Great wine with hors d'oeuvres and fish. To be served at 46 degrees F.

Main places of production:

> San Martino in Colle
> Montecarlo

An appreciable fine table wine is produced in this district with the same variety of grapes, but not selected ones.

It should be pointed out that some vineyards in the village of Veneri, which is in the municipality of Pescia (Pistoia), also form part of the classical production area of the Montecarlo Bianco wine.

Montecarlo Rosso

Grapes of the Sangioveto, Trebbiano, Canaiolo and other varieties.
Suitable for ageing. Garnet red colour, bright; full bouquet.
At first, somewhat rough, becoming dry with age; austere, soft, of good body, harmonious.
Alcohol by vol. 12-13%, total acidity 0.6%.
Il properly matured, it is a great wine with white and red-meat roasts and game. A must with thrush cooked on the spit.

Main places of production:

San Martino in Colle
Montecarlo

PISA

Chianti dei Colli Pisani

Grapes of the Sangioveto, Canaiolo, Malvasia, Trebbiano, and other local varieties.
Suitable for very moderate ageing. Beautiful ruby red colour, pleasant vinous aroma. Dry, tasty, sincere, fresh, smooth, well-balanced.
Alcohol by vol. 11-12%, total acidity 0.6%.
Superior table wine. To be served at room temperature.

Main places of production:

> Capannoli
> Casciana Terme
> Crespina
> Fauglia
> Terricciola

PISTOIA

Chianti Montalbano

Grapes of the Sangioveto (mostly), Trebbiano, Canaiolo, Malvasia varieties.

Suitable for ageing. Deep ruby red colour with violet reflections; typical sweet violet aroma, which deepens with age. Dry taste, soft, strong, harmonious.

Alcohol by vol. 11.5-13.5%, total acidity 0.6-0.75%.

Superior table wine, and, if properly aged, suitable with roasts. To be served at 64 degrees F.

Main places of production:

> Lamporecchio
> Tizzana
> Vinci

Appreciatable white wines are produced in the Pistoian part of Montalbano. They have a golden yellow colour with a pronounced aroma. They are dry and tasty.

SIENA

Moscadello

"So graceful - so heavenly - Moscadelletto - of Montalcino". (Francesco Redi).

Grapes of the Moscadello variety.
Pale golden colour, subtle aroma. Sweet taste, suave, soft; light, sparkling, well-balanced.
Alcohol by vol. 7-8%, total acidity 0.6-0.7%.
Inimitable wine with cakes. To be served at 55 degrees F.

Main place of production:

Montalcino

Vernaccia di San Gimignano also called Vernaccia di Pietrafitta

"... which kisses, licks, bites, thrusts and stings". (Michelangelo Buonarroti the Younger).
Grapes of the Vernaccia variety from San Gimignano.
Suitable for ageing. Pale golden yellow colour, bright; with age it acquires a subtle and penetrating aroma. Dry, with a very pleasing slightly bitter touch, fresh, sustained and good quality, harmonious.
Alcohol by vol. 11-13%, total acidity 0.5-0.6%.
Great wine suitable with fish. To be served at 46 regrees F. A sweet type of this wine is also made but I do not recommend it.

Main place of production:

San Gimignano

Brunello di Montalcino

Grapes of the Brunello variety.
Mature at 5 years, magnificent for ageing (up to 50 years). Deep garnet red colour which improves with the years, changing to orange. Full bouquet, tasty, soft, rich, consistent and fine quality, velvety; full, harmonious.
Alcohol by vol. 13%, total acidity 0.6-0.7%.
Aristocratic wine with roasts, especially with red-meat roasts and all game.

It is the wine I prefer with mixed grills and with various dishes based on fresh goose liver. To be served at 68 degrees F. in elegant rounded glasses of average size and made of pure crystal in order to bring out the qualities of both the bouquet and the colour. The bottles should be uncorked 24 hours before serving.

Main place of production:

Montalcino

Chianti Classico

Grapes of the Sangioveto (mostly), Canaiolo, Trebbiano and Malvasia varieties.

Suitable for ageing. Vivid ruby red colour which tends to become brick red with age, bright; typical bouquet with persistent aroma of sweet violets, violets and irises. Dry, with a very pleasing and slightly bitter after-taste, velvety, austere, full-bodied, of consistent and good quality, harmonious.

Alcohol by vol. 12-13%, total acidity 0.6-0.7%.

Aristocratic wine suitable with roasts; especially with red-meat roasts and all game. To be served at 70 degrees F. in elegant rounded glasses, of average size, and made of pure crystal in order to bring out the qualities of both the bouquet and the colour.

Main places of production:

Castellina in Chianti
Gaiole in Chianti
Radda in Chianti
Greve
San Casciano in Val di Pesa

Besides the classical superior type of bottled Chianti which we have described and which undergoes a preliminary three-year ageing in oak barrels, a fine classical type of Chianti is produced in this classical district, sold in the typical Tuscan presentation, in flasks, but it has less severe organoleptic characteristics.

Chianti dei Colli Senesi

Grapes of the Sangioveto, Trebbiano, Malvasia, Canaiolo and other local varieties.
Suitable for ageing.   Ruby red colour, delicate aroma. Dry, tasty, sincere, soft, harmonious.
Alcohol by vol. 12-13%, total acidity 0.6-0.7%.
Superior table wine and, if properly aged, suitable with roasts. To be served at 65 degrees F.

Main places of production:

> Casole d'Elsa
> Castelnuovo Berardenga
> Colle Val d'Elsa
> Monteriggioni
> Poggibonsi
> San Gimignano
> Siena
> Sinalunga
> Soricille

Vino Nobile di Montepulciano

"Excellent either in Winter or in Summer; the red wine is better in Summer, I am sure. Such wines have bouquet, colour and flavour, and His Holiness drank them with pleasure, not so much in Rome, where they were transported in flasks, but also in Perugia". (Sante Lancerio).
Grapes of the Sangioveto, (mostly), Canaiolo, Malvasia, Trebbiano and other varieties.
Suitable for maturing.   Deep garnet red colour, typical

persistent sweet violet aroma. Rather discordant when young, becoming dry with age with a pleasant, slightly bitter touch, soft; warm, generous.

If properly matured, it is a great wine for white and red-meat roasts and fowl.

To be served at 65 degrees F.

A sweetish type is also produced, but I do not recommend it.

Main place of production:

> Montepulciano

Aleatico

With similar organoleptic characteristics, but with less body, than the classic type from the Island of Elba.

Main places of production:

> Monte Argentario
> Montepulciano
> Orbetello
> Pitigliano

Vin Santo

Golden yellow or amber colour. Sweet, velvety and generous. Particularly appreciatable in the area of the classic Chianti.

Main places of production:

> Montevarchi
> Pescia
> San Gimignano

Malvasia

Golden yellow colour, delicately sweet, particularly appreci-atable in the area of the classic Chianti and at Montegonzi (which is a village in Cavriglia, Arezzo).

Umbria

Marchesi Lodovico & Piero   Antinori ~ Firenze ~ Italy

VILLA ANTINORI
Gran Vino del Chianti

ANTINORI

AZIENDA VITIVINICOLA ELBANA
PORTOFERRAIO (Isola d'Elba)
PROPRIETA' MARCHESI L. &P. ANTINORI

ALEATICO STRAVECCHIO

PRODUZIONE DELLE CANTINE DEI MARCHESI

ANTINORI

TENUTA DI BELVEDERE – Bolgheri (Livorno)

OR.FE.VI.

1873 · 1873

VALTELLINA

AMONG THE BEST RED WINES OF ITALY

INFERNO

FEDEXPORT ITALIA

PRODUCED AND BOTTLED IN ITALY BY

ENOLOGICA VALTELLINESE (Established 1873)

STABILIMENTO DI SONDRIO

NET CONTENTS 1 PT. 8 FL. OZ. - ALC. 12% BY VOL.

OR.FE.VI.

BARDOLINO

PRODUCED AND BOTTLED IN ITALY BY

CANTINE DEL LAGO DI GARDA
FEDERAZIONE ITALIANA DEI CONSORZI AGRARI
NET CONTENTS 1 PT. 8 FL. OZ. - ALC. 11,5 BY VOL.

PERUGIA

Trebbiano

Grapes of the Trebbiano, Spoletino (mostly) and other varieties.
Greenish white colour, very limpid; typical vinous aroma. Dry taste, sincere, but excessively tannic and consequently astringent.
Alcohol by vol. 13%, total acidity 0.7%.
Table wine. To be served at 53 degrees F.

Main place of production:
Montefalco

Sacrantino

Grapes of the Sacrantino variety.
Beautiful garnet red colour, full aroma. Two types are

produced: one is sweetish and the other is sweet, both full and generous.

Alcohol by vol. 13-15%, total acidity 0.6%.

The sweetish type is suitable as a table wine and the sweet one for dessert.

To be served at 62-64 degrees F.

Main place of production:

Montefalco

Scacciadiavoli

Grapes of the Barbera (mostly) and Montepulciano varieties. Ruby red colour, vinous aroma, sweetish taste, strong, fresh but rather high in tannic content, therefore slightly astringent. Alcohol by vol. 13-14%, total acidity 0.8%.

Likeable table wine. To be served at 60 degrees F.

Main places of production:

Giano dell'Umbria
Gualdo Cattaneo
Montefalco

Vernaccia di Cannara

Grapes of the Cornetta variety (an oval type of Barbera grape). Dark, but very clear, red colour, sweet and the wine-making process could be called a "ritual". The grapes are put to dry on a special fruit tray, then pressed in a vat for limited fermentation. They are then subjected to various decantings when the moon changes in order to avoid further fermentation. In March, as a result of this treatment, the Vernaccia becomes perfectly clear and is distributed for consumption. This happens, following an ancient tradition, in the afternoon of Easter Day, on the occasion of a religious ceremony called the "Processione dell' Inchinata" (Procession of Obeisance).

It is a favourite ladies' wine.

Main place of production:

Cannara

TERNI

Orvieto

Pinturicchio liked the Orvieto wine so much that he stipulated in his contract with the people responsible for the building of the Cathedral for his paintings that he should be granted as much Orvieto wine as he could drink. (et vinum quantum libuerit - and as much wine as it pleased him to drink).

Grapes of the Trebbiano (mostly), Verdello, Procanico, Greco and other varieties.

Pale straw colour with golden reflections, bright; delicate typical aroma.

The sweetish type of wine, which is better known, has a pleasantly sweet taste and is of good body.

Alcohol by vol. 11-12%, total acidity 0.6-0.75%.

Superior table wine; recommended with fish and other soups. To be served at 50 degrees F.

The dry type has a delightful acidulous after-taste; it is refreshing, smooth and harmonious.

Great wine with fish. To be served at 48 degrees F.

Main place of production:

Orvieto

Marche

Verdicchio is considered the great King of the Marches; of this there is no doubt and extraordinary tales are told of its glory. It is said that when Hannibal was crossing the Marches with his army of Gallic mercenaries and Carthaginian veterans, he was in danger of seeing his army drunk and at the mercy of the Roman soldiers: fault of the Verdicchio which, on that occasion, was declared an ally of the Romans and honour and great fame was accorded it.

The pilgrims, called at that time the "Romei", who used to come to Rome to gain indulgences, when passing through the Marches stopped at the inns and drank that "wine wich makes the heart beat and gives pleasure to the mind" according to that which one reads in the memoirs of an anonymous "Romeo". But the focal point in the glory of Verdicchio was the birth of Emperor Frederick II at Jesi. His mother, Constance, was in that city when she felt her labour pains commence at a time when a very particular situation was arising: the Empress, a widow, feared

215

that the birth of her son could be disputed as illegitimate by the Sicilian pretenders to the throne; she therefore decided to give birth to her child in public in order to get rid of every doubt regarding the legitimacy of the succession of the child about to be born. In the square was erected a tent in which Frederick II, the "Puer Apuliae", was born, he whom Destiny chose as the symbol of the Empire in the conflict of investitures against the Church. As soon as the imperial baby was born, the followers of Constance exalted; it was a male, the dinasty could continue within its rights and, naturally, as all good Germans, they drank many toasts in the good wine of the region which to-day is called "Verdicchio of the Jesi Castles", a light straw in colour and very clear. This wine has a faint aroma, it is dry with a bitterish taste; specialists, who know how to use the correct terminology for wine, describe it as "fresh, harmonious", according to a specialized nomenclature. However, it is a superior table wine which, after suitable maturing, may be served with fish.

From Hannibal, from Frederick II, to fish — certainly a wonderful, heroic itinerary followed by this wine wich, under different denominations, has run through the history of the Marches from the time of the Piceni till to-day! Verdicchio has wetted — this is the right word — the adventures of all the personalities who found glory and death in the Marches during the past centuries: and this genuine wine has also come to the notice of the poets, who have sung of it as sifted gold, as powdered topaz, as the liqueur of the Gods, and someone has sung of it as the delight of the prelates who, with reason, are considered refined oenologists.

A counter-attraction to Verdicchio in red, Montepulciano del Conero is found in the region of Ancona, ruby red in colour, sometimes dense; a wine of good body, heavy, dry; there are some who define it as austere. Apart from the affectation of this term, which paves the way to images of great severity inconsistent with a happy, pleasant wine such as *Montepulciano del Conero*, it seems that this qualification is rather irreverant to those who are truly austere.

But should you eat a local dish in Pesaro — a sauce of beef with bacon, carrots, celery and cloves — look for a good *Sangiovese Marchigiano*, a perfect red table wine with the aroma of raspberries.

The Marches also produce wines near Pesaro which can enrich any cellar whatsoever and which go under the generical name of red and white *Piceno*. Experts say that, among these wines, there are some worthy of great fame. And the experts must be believed because they are refined oenologists who are anxious to maintain high the prestige of the category, which they defend with an inflexible severity.

The cooking in the Marches is tasty and rich with spices: a fact which is not surprising considering that the Marches were once part of the obligatory road of the cargoes which were carried from the East to Northern Europe; thus spices are at home in the Marches and consequently the wines are very aromatic, full of character and rich in flavour: but always authentic, genuine wines, wines which give a light elation but keep the head clear.

ANCONA

Verdicchio dei castelli di Jesi

Grapes of the Verdicchio (mostly), Biancame, Malvasia and Golden Trebbiano varieties.
Suitable for moderate ageing.   Clear, pale straw colour, very limpid. Subtle aroma. Dry or semi-dry taste with a slightly bitter touch, fresh, harmonious.
Alcohol by vol. 11-13%, total acidity 0.6-07%.
Superior table wine; if properly matured, recommended with fish.
To be served at 50 degrees F.

Main places of production:

> Castelbellino
> Castelplanio
> Cupra montana

Moriolati Spontini
Montecerotto
Rosora
Staffolo

Montepulciano del Conero

Grapes of the Montepulciano and other varieties.
Suitable for maturing. Ruby red colour of varying grades
of deepness, bright; likeable vinous aroma. Tasty, rich in
body, harmonious; if well matured, it is dry and austere.
Alcohol by vol. 11-13%, total acidity 0.7%.
Superior table wine and, if well aged, suitable with white
and red-meat roasts. To be served at room temperature.

Main places of production:

Ancona
Camerano
Castelfidardo
Offogna
Osimo

ASCOLI PICENO

Both red and white wines of a certain value are produced in
wide areas of the province and are called *Red Piceno* and
White Piceno. The white type is of a pale straw colour,
very limpid and aromatic. Dry, tasty, fresh and harmonious.
The red type is of a ruby red colour with varying grades
of deepness, vinous aroma, dry taste, fairly strong, well-
balanced.

Main places of production:

Acquaviva Picena
Appignano del Tronto

Ascoli Piceno
Fermo
Grottammare
Offida
Rapagnano
Sant'Elpidio a Mare

MACERATA

Montesanto

Grapes of the Montepulciano and Sangiovese (mostly) and other varieties.
Beautiful bright ruby red colour; vinous aroma. Sweetish taste, pleasant, harmonious.
Alcohol by vol. 12%, total acidity 0.7-0.8%.
Blends very well with "pisellata" of Monte Lupone, a delicious soup of peas seasoned with bacon.
Good table wine. To be served at slightly below room temperature.

Main places of production:

Civitanova Alta
Montecòsano
Monte Lupone
Morrovalle
Potenza Picena

Vernaccia Spumante di Serrapetrona

Grapes of the Red Vernaccia variety.
Suitable wine for moderate ageing. Deep purple colour, typical aroma.
Sweet taste as soon as it has been bottled; delicately sweet or sweetish at the end of fermentation in the bottles.

Average alcohol by vol. 11.5-13%, total acidity 0.65%.
To be drunk as a dessert wine or between meals. To be
served at room temperature.

Main places of production:

San Severino Marche
Serra Petrona

PESARO - URBINO

Bianchello

Grapes of the Bianchello variety.
Very pale straw colour. Pleasant aroma, dry, with a definite
and marked acidulous touch, not unpleasant.
Alcohol by vol. 10%, total acidity 0.8%.
Table wine. I recommend it with "cannocchie ripiene in
teglia" (stuffed shell-fish cooked in a baking pan).
To be served cool.

Main places of production:

Barchi
Cartoceto
Fano
Mondàvio
Montemaggiore al Metauro
San Giorgio di Pesaro

Sangiovese Marchigiano

Grapes of the Sangiovese variety.
Rather deep ruby red colour, characteristic pleasant raspberry
aroma; dry taste, less tannic and more round than the
Romagnolo type.

Alcohol by vol. 10%, total acidity 0.6%.
Table wine particularly recommended with "pasticciata alla pesarese" (beef stew with bacon, carrots, celery and cloves). To be served at room temperature.

Main places of production:

> Cartoceto
> Fano
> Gradara
> Montebarroccio
> Montelalmate
> Montemaggio
> Pesaro
> Saltara
> Sant'Angelo in Lizzola

OR.FE.VI.

1873 **1873**

VALTELLINA
AMONG THE BEST RED WINES OF ITALY

SASSELLA

PRODUCED AND BOTTLED IN ITALY BY

ENOLOGICA VALTELLINESE (Established 1873)

STABILIMENTO DI SONDRIO

NET CONTENTS 1 PT. 8 FL. OZ. - ALC. 12% BY VOL.

OR.FE.VI.

Valpolicella

PRODUCED AND BOTTLED IN ITALY BY

CANTINE DEL LAGO DI GARDA
FEDERAZIONE ITALIANA DEI CONSORZI AGRARI

NET CONTENTS 1 PT. 8 FL. OZ. - ALC. 11,5 BY VOL.

Viviani: La zuppiera

Lazio

The wines from the Sacco river valley, the Lepini mountains from Valmontone, Artena and Montelanico to Carpineto and Gorga, and those produced on the plains at Latina, Cori, Sezze, Norma and Ninfa, are wines from poor earth. The farmer in these parts has to ask Mother Earth for everything he needs for his livelihood: corn and polenta, figs and melons, wine and red peppers. He is so busy that he is unable to look after his vines very much, in the sense that all he is able to do is press the grapes.

These ordinary wines, which are not very strong but always semi-sparkling and pleasing to the palate, contain a fresh, young taste which makes the drinker feel like a boy again.

Very often a red grape is mixed with the white which gives it sparkle and the perfume of the fields. At Segni the people drink it with chestnuts in the Winter evenings; they call it "caccia e mitti" which means "pour it out and drink it".

The wines from Zagarolo, Genazzano, Palestrina and Paliano should also be remembered. Through industrialization, they have now lost some of their vinous flavour and they do not keep so long.

A stop must be made in the famous area of Cesanese del Piglio and Olevano. Here are the sweet, rich, red wines described by the poet Belli as mellow and so vigorous and velvety that a glass really is a glass. Wines which border on the dry side are not missing and they are among the best. If the white sparkling wine from Olevano could be exported, it would be more appreciated than many other well-known wines.

Rome, the capital of this wine country, is, for this reason, full of inns where the wine from the Roman Castles is generally drunk. However, wines from Montefiascone, Morlupo, Vignanello and Nettuno are also to be found.

Many of these inns have disappeared, giving way to restaurants whose tables, covered with cloths, are filled with foreigners. Some still remain and serve their home cooking on marble tables and some, better known for their wines, serve only bread and salami to accompany them. Their best time is the evening when people gather together "to drink a drop with a friend" and litres, half litres and quarters appear and disappear among the happy voices together with lemonade for the children.

But a stop had been made at Olevano: it is like returning to childhood, roaming amongst the vines in the temperate hours of the day. There are grapes of incredible sweetness, peaches, apricots, figs, and flowers of all kinds; under the bowers at mid-day, tables are laden with egg noodles and roast chicken, ham and "caciotta" cheese, all produced locally and cooked at home.

Inland along the Via Cassia, the land is very poor and it is not for thirty miles that the sourish wines of Sutri and Capranica, Ronciglione and Vetralla are found; and in order to enjoy the pike from Marta it must be accompanied by the wine from Montefiascone.

However, the most well-known wines from Lazio are those produced in the hills around Rome, the so-called Roman Castles, and the most famous is the Frascati wine. But each village makes its own with its peculiar, unmistakable characteristics: Frascati,

Rocca di Papa, Marino, Castel Gandolfo, Albano, Genzano, Nemi. The wine from Frascati has a persistent nutty flavour, that from Velletri is fiery and that from Grottaferrata is pale and the bottles cloud over when taken from the cold cellars. The strong red wines from Marino and also from Velletri are to be drunk with roast meat, but they are rare in an area which produces mainly white wines. At Squarciarelli, the wines are kept underground in labyrinths of cellars in whose walls hundred of vats and barrels, ten and fifteen years of age, are conserved; it is a kind of Holy City of catacombs, excavated for the glory of Trebbiano and other wines from the Castles.

Everywhere there are small shops and stalls which offer appetizers to accompany the drink and whet the desire for more. Here is the ideal place to see what the "porchetta romana", Roman pork, really is, or the slices of dried horse meat covered with red peppers; disdainful people eat bread and salami; those who are not hungry eat doughnuts, biscuits and certain hard, toffee-coloured cakes made of flour, honey and wine which take an hour to eat.

FROSINONE

Cesanese del Piglio

Grapes of the Cesanese variety.

Suitable for ageing; two types are produced.

The first is deep ruby red colour, with a typical aroma and a dry soft taste.

Average alcohol by vol. 11.5%, total acidity 0.6-0.7%.

Good wine, or when properly matured, excellent table wine. It blends very well with a rich dish "timballo di Anagni" (timbale of Anagni), which is said to have been a favourite dish of Pope Boniface VIII. To be served at room temperature. The second type, ruby red colour, with a pronounced characteristic aroma and mellow taste, is velvety and strong.

Dessert wine. To be served at room temperature.

Main places of production:

Acuto
Alatri
Anagni
Fiuggi
Paliano
Piglio
Serrone

LATINA

Falernum

Grapes of the Falanghina variety.
Suitable for moderate ageing. Pale straw colour with greenish reflections, very limpid. Pleasing characteristic aroma. Dry, with an almost imperceptible bitter touch, velvety, harmonious.
Alcohol by vol. 12-13%, total acidity 0.5%.
Excellent table wine and, when properly matured, suitable with fish.
To be served at 50 degrees F.

Main places of production:

Formia
Gaeta

Aleatico di Terracina

Grapes of the Aleatico variety.
Vivid ruby red colour; full and typical aroma. Sweet taste, full, sincere and generous.
Alcohol by vol. 14-15%, total acidity 0.6-0.7%.
Sweet dessert wine. To be served at 64 degrees F.

Main place of production:

Terracina

Cecubo

Grapes of local varieties.
Suitable for ageing. Ruby red colour, pronounced aroma.
Dry taste, soft, with good body, harmonius.
Alcohol by vol. 13-14%, total acidity 0.5%.
Superior table wine and, if well matured, suitable with red
and white-meat roasts. To be served at room temperature.

Main places of production:

Fondi
Formia
Gaeta
Sperlonga

Monte Giove

Grapes of Cesanese variety.
Suitable for ageing. Ruby red colour, very clear; pleasant
vinous aroma which, with age, softens into a delicate aroma
of violets. Dry taste, velvety, harmonious.
Alcohol by vol. 12-14%, total acidity 0.5-0.7%.
Outstanding table wine and, if well aged, suitable with
red and white-meat roasts. To be served at 64 degrees F.
Places of production: Monte Giove, the valley of San Silviano,
the hill of Barchi, and along the coast between Terracina
and Mount Circeo.

ROMA

Castelli Romani

Although I do not agree with everything he says, I will quote
Hans Bart: "We are in our most ideal paradise, in a town

233

full of Temples to Bacchus, in the fairyland of the drinker, where every house is a cellar and an altar of the orgiastic cult, where every stool placed in front of a bowl is a typical tripod. Here is the Kingdom of the God crowned with vine-leaves: the stakes of the vines, like innumerable pyramids of an army's guns, and like an apocalyptic fortress, surround and defend the places of grace, and the perfume of the wine and the sun spread themselves poetically all over this land. Ah, here the true man still lives, as he was born to drink, the cask is his foster-mother and the blood of the God Himself runs in his veins. "Evoé Bacche"! Everything here becomes wine, everything, life and death, thought, sentiment, dreams, love and hate... everything shines in the glass, as the poet sings: It is a mystical revelation, a piece of Olympus fallen to earth, permeated with scintillating celestial breezes, a world of eternal feasts, the truth in the fine veil of poetry, a secret treasure of grace lavished in waves of enchantment". Grapes of the Yellow, Green and Tuscan Trebbiano and White Bonvino varieties.

Frascati

Clear golden yellow colour, pronounced characteristic aroma. Three types are produced: dry, sweetish and sweet. It is always sincere and harmonious. The sweet type, so-called Cannellino, is considered the best wine of the Roman Castles, tasty and velvety.

Average alcohol by vol. 11.5%, total acidity 0.5-0.6%.

Excellent table wine. To be served cool.

Main places of production:

> Frascati
> Grottaferrata
> Monteporzio Catone

Colli Albani

Pale straw colour, clear, delicate characteristic aroma; generally dry taste, full, well-balanced.

Alcohol by vol. 11.5%, total acidity 0.6%.

Good table wine. It blends very well with fried "latterini", small fish from the lake of Albano. To be served cool.

Main places of production:

> Albano Laziale
> Ariccia
> Castel Gandolfo

Colli Lanuvini

Golden yellow colour, pronounced typical aroma, sweetish to the palate, pleasant, full-bodied.

Alcohol by vol. 11.5%, total acidity 0.55%.

Fine table wine, it blends very well with asparagus dishes. To be served cool.

Main place of production:

> Genzano
> Lanuvio

Velletri

Pale straw colour, delicate typical aroma; normally dry taste, with a pleasant slightly bitter touch, full, harmonious.

Alcohol by vol. 11%, total acidity 0.6%.

Good table wine, it blends very well with artichokes "alla matticella", (artichokes marinated in oil and cooked on the embers of vine twigs).

To be served cool.

Main place of production:

> Velletri

Colonna

Golden yellow colour, light typical aroma; dry or sweetish, of fair body.

Average alcohol by vol. 11%, total acidity 0.6%.

Good table wine. Very suitable with "ciriole", small eels from the Tiber and peas. To be served cool.

Main place of production:

Colonna

Marino

Pale straw colour, bright; delicate characteristic bouquet, slightly aromatic due to the prevalence in the district of the Malvasia variety of grapes. Dry with a taste of almonds, tasty, generous.

Alcohol by vol. 12%, total acidity 0.55-0.6%.

Good table wine; it is execellent with a dish of the great cuisine "soupe d'oignon" (onion soup). To be served cool.

Main place of production:

Marino

Aleatico di Genzano

Grapes of the Aleatico variety.

Deep ruby red colour, unmistakable typical aroma which disappears with age. Mellow, soft, well-balanced.

Alcohol by vol. 12-15%, total acidity 0.5-0.7%.

Fruit and dessert wine. To be served cool.

Main place of production:

Genzano

Cesanese di Affile

Grapes of the Cesanese variety.
Suitable for moderate maturing. Two types are produced:
One is deep ruby red colour, of characteristic aroma and dry and soft taste.
Good wine, or, if properly aged, superior table wine. To be served at room temperature.
The second is deep ruby colour, with a pronounced, distinctive aroma and a sweet, velvety taste.
Sweet dessert wine. To be served at room temperature.
Average alcohol by vol. 12%, total acidity 0.6%.

Main places of production:

> Affile
> Arsoli
> Canterano
> Cervara di Roma
> Genazzano
> Olevano Romano
> San Vito Romano
> Subiaco

The Cesanese wines from Marino and Grottaferrata are of good quality, tasty, aromatic, and with a higher alcohol content.

VITERBO

Castrense Bianco

Grapes of the Greco, Romanesco and Malvasia varieties.
Suitable for moderate maturing; it is produced in two types, both of yellowish amber colour and fully flavoured. One is sweetish to the palate, aromatic and sparkling; the other is dry, light and sparkling.

Alcohol by vol. 10%, total acidity 0.5-0.6%.

Good table wine. It is outstanding with the famous "quarantini" which are yellow beans from the grottoes of Castro, cooked quickly and of exquisite taste. To be served cool.

Main places of production:

> Gradoli
> Grotte di Castro

Est! Est! Est!

The sad story of the Abbot Fugger is too well known to be told. I also have had repeated meetings with Est Est Est and, far from dying of it, I have always obtained strength and good humour.

Grapes of the Rossello, Romanesco, Pitino, Procanico, Malvasia and Verdello varieties.

Suitable for moderate ageing. Two types are made:

One has a pale straw colour, bright; full vinous aroma. Dry taste with a pleasant slightly bitter touch.

Excellent table wine and suitable with fish. Blends perfectly with eels, tench and pike, from the lake of Bolsena. To be served at 48 degrees F.

The second type is a very limpid, golden yellow colour, full vinous aroma. Suave and mellow taste. Wine suitable with fruit. To be served at 50 degrees F.

Average alcohol by vol. 9-10%, total acidity 0.35-0.55%.

Main places of production:

> Bolsena
> Montefiascone

A very well-known Vin Santo is produced in Montefiascone.

Vignanello Bianco

"Of all the sparkling wines, this is the most delicious", wrote Barth. Grapes of the Malvasia and Greco varieties.
Pale straw colour, with amber reflections; bright. Light aroma of elder.
Dry taste, slightly salty, sparkling, very pleasant; white froth.
Alcohol by vol. 10%, total acidity 0.5-0.6%.
Good table wine. To be served chilled.

Main places of production:

> Corchiano
> Galure
> Volmano
> Vignanello

Aleatico di Gradoli

Grapes of the Aleatico variety.
Deep ruby red colour, pronounced characteristic aroma. Sweetish, soft, generous, harmonious.
Alcohol by vol. 14-16%, total acidity 0.6%.
Liqueur wine suitable with fruit. To be served cool.

Main places of production:

> Bolsena
> Gradoli
> Grotte di Castro
> Montefiascone

Castrense Rosso

Grapes of the Sangiovese, Canaiolo and Aleatico varieties.
Suitable for moderate maturing. Ruby red colour, bright; vinous aroma, dry taste, pleasant, slightly tannic.
Alcohol by vol. 10-11%, total acidity 0.4%.

Good wine or, if well aged, superior table wine.
To be served at room temperature.

Main places of production:

Gradoli
Grotte di Castro

Vignanello Rosso

Grapes of the Sangiovese, Pinot, Aleatico, Canaiolo and other varieties.
Garnet red colour, bright; full vinous aroma. Dry taste, fresh, smooth.
Alcohol by vol. 11%, total acidity 0.7%.
Fine table wine. To be served at slightly below room temperature.

Main places of production:

Corchiano
Galure
Volmano
Vignanello

Filippo de Pisis: Natura morta con le uova

Abruzzo e Molise

CHIETI

Trebbiano

Grapes of the Trebbiano of the Abruzzi variety.
Variable deepness of golden yellow colour, pleasant aroma.
Dry taste, sincere, pleasing, well-balanced.
Superior table wine to be drunk with fish. Outstanding with
fish soup "alla tiella" - a saucepan - (famous speciality of
Vasto). To be served cold (50 degrees F.).

Main places of production:

> Francavilla
> Giuliano Teatino
> Miglianico
> Montesilvano
> Ortona
> Penne

Pescara
Vasto

Cerasuolo

Grapes of the Montepulciano variety.
Cherry colour, very limpid, full bouquet. Dry taste with a definite sweetish touch, soft, smooth.
Alcohol by vol. 12%, total acidity 0.7%.
Excellent table wine, to be recommended particularly with soups; it is a must with a typical local soup made of diced thistles, turkey livers, pork meat balls and eggs cooked in turkey broth and seasoned with sheep's milk cheese. To be served cool.

Main places of production:

Canosa Sannita
Casoli
Chieti
Penne
Pescara
Popoli
Sulmona
Torre de' Passeri
Vasto

Montepulciano

Grapes of the Montepulciano (mostly) and Sangiovese varieties.
Suitable for moderate ageing. Ruby red colour tending to garnet; pleasing vinous aroma. Dry with distinct sweetish touch not always agreeable; slight red froth.
Alcohol by vol. 12%, total acidity 0.7-0.8%.
Excellent table wine. A must with a sausage called "ventricina" (pork belly and herbs), very tasty and hot.
Produced in the same places as the Cerasuolo wine.

244

Campania

Campania abounds in illustrious and noble wines; the chronicles and stories are full of Falerno, Cecubo and, above all, Greco. Besides, Lazio and Campania were the vines-yards of Rome. The Romans, however, — I mean the ancient Romans at the time of Horace and Apicius — drank a strange and adulterated wine, as different from true wine as that made to the tastes of the Brillat Savarins and the Escoffiers. It is said that the Romans of Petronius's time drank wine a hundred years old: a sort of bitter mush sweetened with honey and cooled with snow.

The real wine of to-day is the same as that of a thousand or two thousand years ago. It is solemn, saintly, like bread, not a liquid to breathe in and to sip. Real wine is a drink; indeed, it is the drink made to quench the thirst, to be drunk at one draught straight out of the bottle.

Beneath a pergola in Terzigno or in Boscotrecase, in the deep shade of the volcano, you may drink all the wine of Vesuvius you like, with figs just picked off the tree, with ham from a thin, black pig, and with home-made macaroni: a wine which really does taste of violets. You may drink the fresh and gay Asprino in the gardens at Terra di Lavoro, with peppers stuffed with macaroni. You may drink the gentle sparkling wine of Lèttere at Gragnano and Castellammare with "parmigiana di melanzane" (aubergines and Parmesan cheese sauce) or with "ziti al ragù" (pasta with meat sauce). You may drink straight from the bottle, just as the day and your thirst demand: you will extract from it joy, deep sleep and good digestion. And an innocent reawakening.

The illustrious Campania, the rich and varied land, which saw the marriage of Rome and Athens, has not, however, only given a vast range of noble wines. It has also given oenologic science to wise men and gastronomes. "Science", if aphorisms of the Salernian School, which were dedicated to drink, may be so called. The mysterious mediaeval doctors and the famous Benedictine monks of the Trinità della Cava said about drink in general: "Drink often, but after meals and, above all, if you want to remain healthy, do not drink during meals".

The doctors from the Salernian School discovered the aperitive value of wine. They prescribed thus: "To keep yourselves healthy, begin your supper with a drink". And: "With every egg, drink a glass of wine". But the most amusing aphorism is that regarding drunkenness: "If the evening libations have ruined you," the monks of Trinità della Cava advised, "drink again in the morning and this will be a medicine for you". However, they warned against drinking wine with a cold: "If your voice is raucous, drink the wine of ducks, that is, water".

In ten verses only, the doctors of the Salernian School defined all the qualities of a good wine. They began like this: "Good wine influences all moods. Black and heavy wine makes one lazy. The wine must be clear, old, shiny, slightly diluted, vivacious and taken in moderation.

Froth is a manifestation of the excellence of the wine.

The goodness of the wine is judged by the aroma, the taste, the clarity and the colour".

248

The Salernian School was a medical establishment formed about 1000 A.D. in the large Benedictine Abbey of Santissima Trinità della Cava near Salerno. The monks had huge estates and they were farmers, industrialists and merchants. Vietri was the port of their little state from which they sent ships to the East to exchange merchandise. They were doctors and surgeons of universal renown, having collected in their monastery the sanitary wisdom of the Greeks, the Latins, the Arabs and the Jews. It was they who looked after and cured Richard the Lion Heart when he was afflicted by a grave wound.

The famous background of this great school of medicine proves the rightness and authority of the precepts of wine elaborated by the school in the first centuries of this millennium. That these precepts were heard and taken note of in Campania, especially by him who was concerned with sincerity and moderation, can be proved by the fact that no other Italian region is so rich in home-made wines, and none so abundant in wines while having so few drunken people.

Drunkenness is as rare, in Campania, as the tap-rooms are many: those popular, rough and simple taprooms which have a branch and a red flag as their sign. The inauguration, the presentation of a taproom in Naples was carried out according to an ancient rite. The opening of a new locality was solemnly proclaimed in all the squares of the village or the district by a "pazzariello" who is a sort of caricature, or imitator of a town-crier. This man dressed in an old, showy livery, a concierge's uniform or one cast off by an officer; on his head he put a cocked hat or tricorn; in his hand he carried a drum-major's stick with a brass head and in his right hand, a flask of new wine. This wretch, in his grotesque general's uniform, was followed by three youths, in corduroy trousers and red and straw colour striped shirts, armed with shepherds' pipes, cymbals and large drums.

These four people, in turn followed by a train of youths, urchins and guttersnipes, went to a square where, after having made a terrible noise with their instruments, the "pazzariello"

249

began to proclaim the wine. In rough dialect verses, each one emphasized by a noise from the band, the town-crier started to announce the opening of a new taproom: he told who was the owner, he indicated the street in which the new tavern was situated and the number of the street; he praised the host and his wine: he distributed sips for the on-lookers to taste; and finally he put himself at the head of the procession, composed of all the rabble and led them, with his crazy trio of musicians, dancing and leaping in front of them all.

One cannot truly say that Neapolitan songs of three centuries ago did not know commercial advertising and did not have the zest of public relations.

AVELLINO

Fiano

Grapes of the Fiano variety.
Suitable for moderate ageing. Rather deep straw colour; subtle aroma which reminds one of Muscat.
Alcohol by vol. 11-12%, total acidity 0.6-0.7%.
Superior table wine to be drunk with fish (particularly trout).
To be served cold (50 degrees F.).

Main places of production:

Atripalda
Avellino
Bellizzi Irpino

Greco di Tufo

Grapes of the Greco of Vesuvius variety.

Suitable for moderate ageing. Golden yellow colour, bright; typical, deep, "sui generis" aroma. Produced in two types: one dry and the other sweetish.

Both fresh, very pleasant and with a slightly scorched taste. Alcohol by vol. 12-13%, total acidity 0.8%.

The dry type is an excellent table wine, and is particularly good with fish, if well matured. The sweetish type is a dessert wine and is very good indeed with "priests' chestnuts"; these are well dried, threaded on string and heated in the oven.

Main places of production

Altavilla Irpino
Lapio
Tufo

Aglianico

Grapes of the Aglianico variety.

Suitable for maturing; deep ruby red colour; fresh and fragrant vinous aroma which ages to a true, lasting bouquet of morello cherries and violets. Somewhat rough and discordant when young (because of excess tannin), becoming tasty, soft and pleasant with age.

Alcohol by vol. 12-13%, total acidity 0.5-0.6%.

Table wine; but, when properly aged, a wine for roasts. When young, to be served at a temperature slightly below average; when matured, at 60 degrees F.

Main places of production:

Monte Pièdame
Santa Paolina
Tufo

Taurasi

Grapes of the Aglianico variety.

Mature in one year, perfect after four and over; suitable for long ageing (even 15 years).

Deep ruby red colour, which tends to brick red with age, vinous aroma which also changes with age; pronounced bouquet of morello cherries and violets.

When young, Taurasi wine is rough and tart, slowly becoming austere, velvety, full and well-balanced.

Alcohol by vol. 12-13%, total acidity 0.7%.

Good table wine; but, when well aged, becomes a great wine with red-meat roasts and all game. It is the best wine to accompany wild boar dishes.

Main places of production:

> San Mango sul Calore
> Sant'Angelo all'Esca
> Taurasi

The production of an appreciable Sangiovese in the municipality of Avellino is worth metioning. This wine is also very alcoholic: 14% by vol. A special cooked wine, called Acinato, is prepared in the province of Avellino. Also worth mentioning is a pleasant wine called Asprino, greenish white in colour, light, acidulous and sparkling which is produced in Mercogliano, Monteforte Irpino and Ospedaletto di Alpìnolo.

BENEVENTO

Solopaca Bianco

Grapes of the Trebbiano, Greco and Malvasia varieties.
Suitable for moderate maturing. Golden yellow colour, bright; pronounced aroma. Dry taste, soft, smooth.
Alcohol by vol. 12%, total acidity 0.6-0.7%.

Good table wine, extremely appreciated with the local "fusilli al sugo", which is a spiral pasta with sauce.
If properly aged, also suitable with fish. To be served at 50 degrees F.

Main places of production:

Castelvenere
Sant'Agata dei frati
Solopaca

Solopaca Rosso

Grapes of the Aglianico, Sangiovese, Olivella, Mangiaguerra and Aleatico varieties.
Suitable for moderate ageing. Deep ruby red colour, full bouquet. Somewhat rough and discordant taste becoming pleasant and velvety with age.
Alcohol by vol. 11-13%, total acidity 0.7%.
Good table wine. To be served at slightly below room temperature.

Main places of production:

Castelvenere
Sant'Agata dei frati
Solopaca

CASERTA

Asprino

"Asprino wine comes from a place near Naples. The best quality, however, originates in Aversa, a unique and good city. It is a healthy drink in Summer. His Holiness sometimes drank of this wine to quench his thirst and relax his body before going to sleep. In order to savour its perfection, it must be fragrant, golden and not absolutely rough. In order to drink it in Summer, it should be put in the cellar in the Spring and it should be so rough that the heat will mtaure it, but first of all the colour should be examined. Such wines are so appreciated even by the inn-keepers that ladies and gentlemen willingly visit them in order to consume 'una foglietta' (half a litre)". (Sante Lancerio).

Grapes of the Asprino variety.

To be consumed within the year. Greenish white colour, very limpid; light aroma. Light, sparkling, tasting of herbs, thirst-quenching, diuretic.

Alcohol by vol. 6-9%, total acidity 0.9-1%.

It is not really a table wine, but a wine to be drunk on hot Summer afternoons. It also blends extraordinarily well with the classic Neapolitan pizza and with tasty dishes prepared with eels and pike. To be served cool 50 degrees F.).

Main places of production:

> Aversa
> Trentola

Falerno Bianco

Grapes of the Falanghina variety.

Suitable for moderate ageing. Pale straw colour with amber reflections, pleasant characteristic aroma. Dry, with a not unpleasant slightly scorched taste, full, likeable.

Alcohol by vol. 12-13%, total acidity 0.5-0.6%.

Excellent table wine and, if properly aged, to be served with fish, above all with fish soups, amongst which is the local "zuppa alla marinara" (a simple fisherman's soup). To be served at 50 degrees F.

Main place of production.

Mondragone

Conca

Grapes of the Sangiovese, Canaiolo, Barbera, Malvasia, Montepulciano and Trebbiano varieties.
Vivid ruby red colour, full vinous aroma. Dry taste with a pronounced sweetish touch, slightly astringent.
Alcohol by vol. 11-13%, total acidity 0.5-0.6%.
Good table wine. To be served at slightly below room temperature.

Main places of production:

Conca della Campania
Galluccio

Falerno Rosso

Grapes of the Aglianico, Strepparossa, Barbera, Durcina and Marsigliese varieties.
Suitable for ageing. Intense ruby red colour, bright; distinctive aroma. Dry taste, slightly austere, warm, full, well-balanced.
Alcohol by vol. 12-13%, total acidity 0.5%.
Excellent table wine and, when well matured, suitable with red-meat roasts. Oustanding with the very famous local game, particularly with "mallardi" (wild duck). To be served at room temperature.
A sweet type is also produced which is not to be recommended.

Main place of production:

Mondragone

256

TRADE MARK

LEONE

Valpolicella

FOLONARI

SUPERIOR RED ITALIAN WINE

PRODUCED IN OUR CELLARS
OF NEGRAR VALPOLICELLA

PRODUCT OF ITALY

Fratelli Folonari S.p.A.

BRESCIA (ITALY)

SINCE 1825

PRODUZIONE   PREGIATA

LISON ROSE'

VINI TIPICI DEL VENETO ORIENTALE

Tenuta S. Margherita

FOND. AGRICOLA IND. S.p.A.
VILLANOVA - PORTOGRUARO

ALCOOL 12% CA.

CONT. ML. 720 CA.

VALDO

TRADE MARK

PROSECCO

PREGIATO · AMABILE

A FERMENTAZIONE NATURALE, OTTENUTO DALLA
SELEZIONE DELLE MIGLIORI UVE DELLA ZONA CLASSICA

VALDO S.A.S. - VALDOBBIADENE

LONGO E ZOPPELLI - TREVISO

TENUTA S. MARGHERITA

Rubino del Piave

VINO PRODOTTO ED IMBOTT. IN ITALIA DALLE

Cantine S. Margherita

FONDIARIA AGRICOLA IND. S.p.A.
VILLANOVA - PORTOGRUARO

ALCOOL 12% IN VOLUME

CONT. Lt. 0.710 CA.

Capri Bianco

Grapes of the Greco and Fiano varieties.
Suitable for ageing. Pale straw colour, bright; subtle aroma. Dry taste with a light but not unpleasant touch of scorched wine, fresh, likeable.
Alcohol by vol. 12.5%, total acidity 0.5-0.7%.
Superior table wine and, if properly matured, suitable with fish. To be served at 50 degrees F.

Main place of production:

Isle of Capri

A Capri Rosso (Red Capri) is also produced: it is a fine table wine.

Ischia Bianco

Grapes of the Biancolella (mostly), Forastera, with Lunarda and Arilla varieties, in smaller proportions.
Suitable for moderate ageing. Deep straw colour, full bouquet. Dry, with a pleasant slightly burnt taste, velvety, full, well-balanced.
Alcohol by vol. 11-13, total acidity 0.5%.
Great wine to be served with fish. To be served at 50 degrees F.

Main places of production:

Forio
Lacco Ameno
Serrara Fontana

The Biancolella and Forastera varieties of grapes, when

processed alone, make the dry, white types of wine called Biancolella and Forastera.

Lacrima Christi del Vesuvio Bianco

Grapes of the Fiano and Greco di Torre varieties.

Suitable for ageing. Pale straw colour with amber reflections, subtle aroma. Dry, with a not unpleasant taste of scorched wine, soft, fresh, harmonious.

Alcohol by vol. 12%, total acidity 0.7-0.8%.

Excellent table wine and, when well matured, suitable with fish. To be served cold (48 degrees F.).

Main places of production:

    Resina
    Torre del Greco

Gragnano

Grapes of the Aglianico, Strepparossa, Iaculillo, Nufriello and Cascaveglia varieties.

Suitable for moderate ageing. Dark garnet red colour, pleasant aroma of faded violets. Sweetish flavour, tasty, moderately alcoholic, sparkling.

Alcohol by vol. 11-12%, total acidity 0.5-0.6%.

Good table wine. To be served at slightly below room temperature.

Main places of production:

    Casola di Napoli
    Gragnano
    Pimonte

Ischia Rosso

Grapes of the Guarnaccia, Strepparossa and Ischia Precoce varieties.

Suitable for ageing. Ruby red colour, delicate aroma. Dry taste, sincere, mellow, well-balanced.
Alcohol by vol. 12.5-13.5%, total acidity 0.6%.
Excellent table wine and, if properly matured, suitable with white and red-meat roasts.
Produced in the Isle of Ischia.

Lacrima Christi del Vesuvio Rosso

Grapes of the Aglianico, Strepparossa and Soricella varieties. Suitable for maturing. Deep ruby red colour, subtle aroma which changes to a full bouquet in the course of time. Dry taste, sincere, fresh.
Alcohol by vol. 11-12%, total acidity 0.6%.
Superior table wine; if well matured, suitable with white-meat roasts.
To be served at room temperature.

Main places of production:

> Resina
> Torre del Greco
> Boscoreale

A rosé Lacrima Christi is also produced, which has a sweetish flavour, is fragrant and harmonious.

Vesuvio Rosso

Grapes of the Aglianico, Strepparossa, Catalanesca and Soricella varieties.
Suitable for moderate ageing. Red violet colour, subtle aroma of violets. Dry taste, sincere, sparkling, pleasant. Lively froth.
Alcohol by vol. 10-11%, total acidity 0.5-0.6%.
Good table wine. To be served at slightly below room temperature.

Main places of production:

> San Giuseppe Vesuviano
> Ottaviano
> Terzigno

A Vesuvio Bianco is also produced in the same district, it has a beautiful, clear straw colour, a subtle aroma and a sufficiently dry taste which has a not always pleasant touch of scorched wine. Its alcohol content is very variable according to the years of production (9-13% by vol.). It is a good table wine.

A sparkling Asprino wine is produced in numerous places of the province, the organoleptic characteristics of which have been already described under the wines of the province of Caserta. Particularly appreciatable is the type of wine from Frattamaggiore.

SALERNO

Gran Furor Divina Costiera Bianco

Grapes of the Trebbiano, Finile, Moschella and Ginestra varieties.

Suitable for moderate ageing. One type is of an amberish white colour and another almost white or, properly speaking, white gold; both have a light aroma, are subtly sweetish to the palate, but the first one is more mellow and the second more delicate.

Alcohol by vol. 12-13%, total acidity 0.5-0.6%.

Outstanding wine to be served with fish. To be served at 50 degrees F.

Main place of production:

> Furore

Ravello Bianco

Grapes of the various local varieties.

Suitable for moderate ageing. Pale straw colour, with amber reflections, typical bouquet "sui generis" in which a touch of gentian can be detected. Dry taste, fresh, smooth, harmonious.

Alcohol by vol. 12-13%, total acidity 0.6-0.7%.

Excellent table wine and, if properly aged, suitable with fish. To be served at 50 degrees F.

Main place of production:

Ravello

A white type of wine is also produced, which is delicately sweet, sparkling and exquisite with "sproccolati", which are dried figs threaded on a stick, sprinkled with seeds of fennel and flavoured with bay leaves. A Muscat wine, very aromatic, semi-sweet and alcoholic, is also produced.

Calore degli Alburni

Grapes of the Aglianico, Strepparossa and Sangiovese varieties. Suitable for ageing. Deep ruby red colour, full bouquet. Dry, scorched taste, full, generous.

Alcohol by vol. 12-14%, total acidity 0.6-0.7%.

Good table wine and, if properly matured, suitable with fowl. To be served at room temperature.

Main places of production:

Aquara
Castelcivita
Postiglione

Gran Furor Divina Costiera Rosso

Grapes of the Piede Palumbo, Aglianico, Tronda and Olivella varieties.

261

Suitable for moderate maturing. Beautiful garnet red colour, full bouquet of raspberries and violets. Sweetish to the palate, with a light and pleasant acidulous touch, very likeable. Alcohol by vol. 13%, total acidity 0.65%.

Excellent table wine and, if of a good vintage year, suitable with roasts. To be served at 60 degrees F.

Main place of production:

Furore

A rosé type is also produced which I do not recommend.

Ravello Rosato

Grapes of local and French varieties.

Suitable for moderate ageing. Pink colour, typical bouquet of violets and raspberries. Mellow taste, oily, very pleasant. Alcohol by vol. 12%, total acidity 0.65%.

Dessert wine, to be served also with fruit. To be served at 50 degrees F.

Main place of production:

Ravello

Ravello Rosso

Grapes of the Aglianico, Serpentario and Mangiaguerra varieties.

Suitable for ageing. Ruby red colour, characteristic flavour of old wine.

Dry, with a light sweet after-taste, soft, full, pleasant. Alcohol by vol. 12%, total acidity 0.7%.

Excellent table wine and, if properly matured, suitable with white-meat roasts and fowl. To be served at room temperature.

Main place of production:

Ravello

Puglia

In the dialect of Bari, wine is called "mjere", which is derived from the Latin word "merum" meaning pure, genuine, powerful.

The pure wine from Puglia has remained plebian because it has a definite unsophisticated taste and odour with no nuances. In other words, it is a strong, full-bodied wine which tastes only of grapes. It is sweet or sour depending on the type of grapes which are pressed. As wine it is as genuine as a man, in comparison, should always be masculine and a woman always feminine. No shades of meaning or diplomatic phrases are needed to describe the wine of Puglia which is proud to be what it is, like that blacksmith in Rimbaud's poem, who forced the red beret of the Revolutionists, with great contempt, onto the head of the trembling Louis XVI. It is as strong as a blacksmith of bygone days, strong and black, and it makes the tongue smack against the palate like the vibrating sound of a hammer striking on the anvil.

Its vocabulary is as poor as that of the farmers who drink it; it is therefore classified either as black or as white. These simple descriptions are made in order to distinguish one type from another easily, without taking into account that shade of smoke which seems to veil the shining light of certain white ones, and the reddish colours, like those of cardinals' robes or the plaits of young girls, in the black ones. It is a deep violet, oily, dark, almost a liquid velvet which gives off opaque reflections, which leaves a mark on the lips and which stains the insides of the clay carafes emptied by the labourers on Sundays in the dark tap-rooms of the villages.

It is the wine of a great civilisation, solemn and dramatic like that of Puglia, the wine with the severity of Castel del Monte, of the Romanesque cathedrals, of the Madonna with the black face. It is the tenacius and strong wine of the men of Puglia who have seen Greeks, Swabians and Aragons in their land and who have passed from feudal system to feudal system, unscathed, unbent, immutable, sincere, as are, in fact, the wines of Cerignola, San Severo, Andria, Trani, Barletta, Locorotondo, Conversano, Alberobello, San Pietro Vernotico, Sava, Tricarico and of all the villages of Puglia where the low vine, clinging to the arid soil, accompanies the high, silvery waves of the olive trees, on the plains or on the slopes of the hills, or along the Adriatic coast.

The people are sober drinkers; only on feast days, when the villages are alight with fire-works and the bands play Rossini and Donizetti in the squares, are the voices of the merry peasants heard as they play their traditional game, competing in a severe ritual for glasses of wine. Puglia, the great cellar of Italy, has no drunkards.

The wine is a source of wealth which the people approach with awe, with reluctant avarice. Perhaps, however, it is a sense of respect, of reverence towards the most glorious fruit of the earth; and here the discussion could be carried to the usual theme of paganism which is always evoked when wine is mentioned.

Even if the men are sober, the atmosphere during the grape-harvest is heavy with excitement; then all Puglia is perfumed

266

with wine. The hiss of the fermentation can almonst be heard. There is a holiday feeling in the air.

The labourers, both men and women, have calm faces and bright eyes. While eating their bread and salted sardines, offered by the land-owner, they drink wine and seem to forget, for a while, their poverty.

Then, enclosed in the great cement and glass vats, the must, impregnated with sugar, bubbles fiercely and the perfume, which previously enveloped all the villages of Puglia, is concentrated, like a stupefying aura, around the wineries. In mid-Nocember, however, when the first, rather weak wine — although the alcohol content is always 10% — is tapped, the perfume invades the streets again, but this time it is sweetish, homely, undeveloped and mixes in the air with the smell of figs and almonds cooked together in the ovens which are fed with kindling.

The "mjere" is a great traveller; it loves the railways and, as the men of its native land desire to go North, so the wine of Puglia, every day of the year, leaves northward-bound, closed in huge cisterns which are dirty from the smoke. It leaves with its 15-16% of alcohol content and when it arrives at its destination the oenologists are waiting to cut and emasculate it.

For some time now, however, some courageous and meritorius industrialists in Puglia have tried to wean it from its dialect, to teach it some modern rules, to make of it a "finished product", as it is said in industrial terms. Their initiative is praiseworthy but the real wine of Puglia, the ancient "merum", is still simply that which leaves a stain on the lips and which is drunk in the dark tap-rooms of the villages behind red cotton curtains.

BARI

Bianco di Locorotondo

Grapes of the White Alessano (50%) and Verdea (50%) varieties.

Suitable for ageing. Watery or pale green colour, vinous aroma; dry taste, neutral, nervous.

Alcohol by vol. 10-12%, total acidity 0.45-0.55%.

This wine is mainly used as a base for the making of Vermouth and for blending with countless red and white wines. It deserves a better lot as it should be considered an outstanding table wine and, when well aged, suitable with fish. I had the chance not long ago to taste a 10-year-old bottle with one of Luigi Carnacina's dishes, which was a fillet of sole "alla Casina delle Rose" (a Roman restaurant) and I must say it was matchless. To be served cold (50 degrees F.).

Main places of production:

> Alberobello
> Locorotondo

Moscato di Trani

Grapes of the Muscat variety.
Suitable for ageing. Golden yellow colour, bright. Distinct aroma, typical of the grape added to faded roses. Delicately sweet taste, velvety, warm, oily, full, harmonious.
Alcohol by vol. 16-18% degrees, total acidity 0.6%.
Dessert wine. To be served cool.

Main places of production:

> Andria
> Barletta
> Trani

Verdea

Grapes of the Verdea variety.
Watery colour, subtle persistent bouquet, mellow, sincere, sparkling.
Alcohol by vol. 11-12%, total acidity 0.5-0.55%.
Wine to be served between meals.
To be served cool (50 degrees F.).

Main places of production:

> Alberobello
> Gravina di Puglia
> Noci

Aleatico di Puglia

Grapes of the Aleatico variety.
Suitable for ageing. Vivid garnet red colour which loses strength with age, becoming orange. Exuberant and pleasant

aromatic bouquet; sweet taste, velvety, sincere, full, harmonious.
Alcohol by vol. 15-17%, total acidity 0.6%.
Dessert wine. To be served cool.

Main places of production:

Acquaviva delle Fonti
Barletta
Conversano

Barletta

Grapes of the Uva di Troia (90%), Lagrima (5%) and Montepulciano (5%) varieties.
Purplish red colour, vinous aroma and taste, neutral, warm, full, vigorous.
Alcohol by vol. 14-16%, total acidity 0.5-0.7%.
Wine used for blending with other wines.

Main places of production:

Barletta
Canosa di Puglia
Trani

Castel del Monte Rosato

Grapes of the Black Bombino (70%) and Montepulciano (30%) varieties.
Pink colour, very limpid; delicate aroma of ripe fruit. Round taste, soft, pure.
Alcohol by vol. 11-12%, total acidity 0.55%.
Good table wine. To be served rather cool.

Main places of production:

Andria
Corato
Ruvo di Puglia

A white wine called Castel del Monte Bianco is also produced in this area in smaller quantities. This wine has a pale yellow colour, a typical subtle and persistent aroma and a dry and soft taste.

Castel del Monte Rosso

Grapes of the Black Bombino (70%), Montepulciano (15%) and Uva di Troia (15%) varieties.
Suitable for ageing. Beautiful deep ruby red colour, vinous aroma typical of the grape; dry, sincere, smooth.
Alcohol by vol. 11-12%, total acidity 0.5%.
Good table wine, when well aged suitable with meat roasts. To be served at room temperature.

Main places of production:

> Andria
> Corato
> Ruvo di Puglia

Primitivo di Gioia del Colle

Grapes of the Primitivo di Gioia variety either alone or mixed with 10% of the Zingarello variety.
Purplish red colour, vinous aroma; vinous taste, sweetish to the palate, warm, full, vigorous.
Alcohol by vol. 15-17%, total acidity 0.65-0.75%.
Several types of this wine are made: wines with a high percentage of alcohol suitable for blending with lighter wines and, above all, also a table wine made from the hidden grapes of the bunch which mature later and are processed separately. Finally, after various blendings and consequent gradual ageing lasting from 5 to 15 years, a wine is obtained which, little by little, loses its colour and becomes orange, and which acquires, according to the years of ageing, such qualities that it must be considered suitable with red and

TRADE   MARK

LEONE

Valpolicella

FOLONARI

SUPERIOR RED ITALIAN WINE

PRODUCED IN OUR CELLARS
OF NEGRAR VALPOLICELLA

PRODUCT OF ITALY

Fratelli Folonari S.p.A.

BRESCIA (ITALY)

SINCE 1825

PRODUZIONE   PREGIATA

LISON ROSE'

VINI TIPICI DEL VENETO ORIENTALE

Tenuta S. Margherita

FOND. AGRICOLA IND. S.p.A.
VILLANOVA - PORTOGRUARO

ALCOOL 12% CA.   CONT. ML. 720 CA.

VALDO

TRADE MARK

PROSECCO

PREGIATO · AMABILE

A FERMENTAZIONE NATURALE, OTTENUTO DALLA
SELEZIONE DELLE MIGLIORI UVE DELLA ZONA CLASSICA

VALDO S.A.S. - VALDOBBIADENE

LONGO E ZOPPELLI - TREVISO

TENUTA S. MARGHERITA

Rubino del Piave

VINO PRODOTTO ED IMBOTT. IN ITALIA DALLE

Cantine S. Margherita

FONDIARIA AGRICOLA IND. S.p.A.
VILLANOVA - PORTOGRUARO

ALCOOL 12% IN VOLUME

CONT. Lt. 0.710 CA.

PRODUCT OF ITALY
Melini
ETICHETTA   DEPOSITATA
FORNITRICE
CANTINE in PONTASSIEVE   FORNITRICE   E CASTELLINA in CHIANTI   FORNITRICE di S.A.R.
CASA FONDATA
NEL 1705   56 MASSIME
ONORIFICENZE
DELLA R.CASA   IL DUCA D'AOSTA
DI S.M. LA REGINA MADRE E DI S.S.P.P. PIO X
PRODUCED AND BOTTLED BY ANTICA CASA VINICOLA
TOSCANA CAV. A. LABOREL MELINI · PONTASSIEVE (FIRENZE)
CONTENTS   ALCOHOL BY
1 QUART   VOLUME 12½%
CHIANTI
PRINTED IN ITALY

PRODUCT OF ITALY
Melini
ETICHETTA   DEPOSITATA
FORNITRICE
CANTINE in PONTASSIEVE   FORNITRICE   E CASTELLINA in CHIANTI   FORNITRICE di S.A.R.
CASA FONDATA
NEL 1705   56 MASSIME
ONORIFICENZE
DELLA R.CASA   IL DUCA D'AOSTA
DI S.M. LA REGINA MADRE E DI S.S.P.P. PIO X
PRODUCED AND BOTTLED BY ANTICA CASA VINICOLA
TOSCANA CAV. A. LABOREL MELINI · PONTASSIEVE (FIRENZE)
CONTENTS 1 PINT AND   ALCOHOL BY
7 FLUID OUNCES   VOLUME 12.5%
ORVIETO
PRINTED IN ITALY

OR. FE. VI.
Rosato del
CONERO
CONSORZIO AGRARIO PROVINCIALE
DI ANCONA

Rosatello
VIN ROSE

BOTTLED BY
I.L. RUFFINO
PONTASSIEVE (ITALY)

NOME E RECIPIENTE DEPOSITATO

NET CONTENTS 1 QUART
PRODUCT OF ITALY
ALCOHOL BY VOLUME 12°

I.L. RUFFINO

CHIANTI WINE
Esportazione Vinicola Toscana

I.L. RUFFINO
PONTASSIEVE (FIRENZE)
40 MASSIME ONORIFICENZE
ESPOSIZIONI MONDIALI

FORNITORI DELLA REAL CASA D'ITALIA

FORNITORI DEI SACRI PALAZZI APOSTOLICI

PRODUCT OF ITALY · NET CONTENTS 1 QUART · ALCOHOL BY VOL. 13%

VERDICCHIO
DEI CASTELLI DI JESI

CONSORZIO AGRARIO   PROVINC. DI ANCONA

FEDEXPORT ITALIA

Rosatello
VIN ROSE

BOTTLED BY
I. L. RUFFINO
PONTASSIEVE (ITALY)

NOME E RECIPIENTE DEPOSITATO

NET CONTENTS 1 QUART
PRODUCT OF ITALY
ALCOHOL BY VOLUME 12º

I. L. RUFFINO
CHIANTI WINE
Esportazione Vinicola Toscana
I. L. RUFFINO
PONTASSIEVE (FIRENZE)
40 MASSIME ONORIFICENZE
ESPOSIZIONI MONDIALI

FORNITORI
DELLA REAL CASA D'ITALIA

FORNITORI D.LI
SACRI PALAZZI APOSTOLICI

MARCA DEPOSITATA
PRODUCT OF ITALY · NET CONTENTS 1 QUART · ALCOHOL BY VOL. 13%
REGISTERED IN THE U.S.A. PATENT OFFICE

VERDICCHIO
DEI CASTELLI DI JESI
CONSORZIO AGRARIO   PROVINC. DI ANCONA

FEDEXPORT
ITALIA

MIRAFIORE

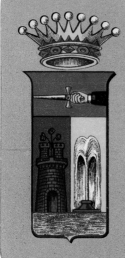

BAROLO

TENIMENTI DI BAROLO E SERRALUNGA D'ALBA

MIRAFIORE CANELLI (ITALIA)

FERRARI

NET CONTENTS
1 PINT 8 FL.OZS

ALCOHOL 12%
BY VOLUME

SOAVE

BIANCO SUPERIORE
ITALIAN DRY WHITE WINE
PRODUCED AND BOTTLED AT
LAZISE SUL GARDA - VERONA
BY
Casa Vinicola Bruno Ferrari s.a.s.
DOSIMO - ITALY

FERRARI

NET CONTENTS
1 PINT 8 FL.OZS

ALCOHOL 12%
BY VOLUME

BARDOLINO
EXTRA SUPERIORE
ITALIAN DRY RED WINE
PRODUCED AND BOTTLED AT
LAZISE SUL GARDA - VERONA
BY

Casa Vinicola Bruno Ferrari s.a.s.

DOSIMO - ITALY

VECCHIO VINO
di
BARBARESCO
ANTICO PODERE CONTI della CREMOSINA

Dr. Arturo Bersano Nizza Monferrato (Asti · Italia)

white-meat roasts; austere, somewhat bitter, mellow, and even a dessert wine.

Main places of production:

Castellana Grotte
Gioia del Colle
Santeramo in Colle

BRINDISI

Malvasia di Brindisi

Grapes of the Malvasia variety.
Pale straw colour, pronounced aroma; dry taste with a distinct sweet touch, smooth, harmonious.
Alcohol by vol. 13.5-14%, total acidity 0.5-0.55%.
Superior table wine, excellent with fish soup and with highly flavoured fish dishes. To be served at 50 degrees F.

Main place of production:

Brindisi

FOGGIA

San Severo Bianco

Grapes of the Bombino variety.
Suitable for moderate ageing. Pale straw colour, with very limpid greenish reflections; light aroma. Dry taste, sincere, light, fresh.
Alcohol by vol. 11.5-12.5%, total acidity 0.55%.
Good table wine. To be served at 50 degrees F.
Produced in the area of San Severo.

A beautiful pink type is also produced in the same area; it has a lively colour, a typical aroma and a dry and harmonious taste.

Primitivo di Bari

Grapes of the Primitivo di Gioia variety.
It has the same organoleptic characteristics as the Primitivo di Gioia of the province of Bari. It is sold only as a wine of high alcohol content for blending with lighter types.

Main places of production:

> Gallipoli
> Squinzano
> Trepuzzi

Rosato of Salento

Grapes of the Negramaro and Malvasia varieties.
Red cherry colour, very limpid; pleasant aroma; tasty, fresh, generous, harmonious.
Alcohol by vol. 12-13%, total acidity 0.65%.
Good table wine; some types are outstanding table wines and really excellent when served with salami.
To be served rather cool (60 degrees F.).

Main places of production:

> Cosentino
> Salice Salentino

LECCE

Squinzano

Grapes of the Negramaro and Malvasia varieties.

Violet red colour, vinous aroma and taste, neutral, warm, full, vigorous.

Alcohol by vol. 15-17, total acidity 0.5-0.6%.

It is also called Doppio Rosso (Double Red) on account of the strength of its colour. It is used for blending with light wines.

Main places of production:

> Campi Salentina
> Nardò
> Squinzano

TARANTO

Bianco di Martina Franca

Grapes of the Verdea and Bianco d'Alessano varieties.

Suitable for moderate maturing. Greenish white or whitish straw colour. Light, almost non-existent aroma. Dry taste, neutral, nervous.

Alcohol by vol. 11-12%, total acidity 0.55%.

The use of this wine, like the Bianco of Locorotondo, is mainly as a base for Vermouth and as a blending element in the processing of innumerable lighter red and white wines. It deserves a better lot as it should be considered an excellent table wine and, if properly aged, suitable with fish. It blends extremely well with "fave calde", hot mashed broad beans, a famous local speciality. To be served cold (50 degrees F.).

Main places of production:

> Martina Franca
> Massafra
> Montemèsola

Primitivo di Manduria

Grapes of the Primitivo di Gioia variety.
Purple red colour, vinous aroma. Sweetish to the palate, warm, full-bodied, vigorous; lasting deep red froth.
Alcohol by vol. 17-18%, total acidity 0.7%.
The same thing may be said of this wine as of the Primitivo di Gioia del Colle. Most of the production is used for blending purposes, which is a great pity because, through gradual ageing lasting from 3 to 8 years, a wine is obtained which, little by little, loses its colour and becomes orange, and which acquires, according to the years of maturation, such qualities that it must be considered suitable with red and white-meat roasts; austere, somewhat bitter, soft and even suitable as a dessert wine.

Main places of production:

> Fragagnano
> Mandunia
> Maruggio

Primitivo del Tarantino

Grapes of the Primitivo di Gioia (mostly) and other black varieties (Black Moscato, Black Malvasia, Negro Amaro).
Purplish red colour, vinous aroma. Mellow or sweet taste, full-bodied, warm, strong.
Alcohol by vol. 15-17%, total acidity 0.6-0.65%.

Main places of production:

> Carosino
> Grottaglie
> Monteparano

Lucania

POTENZA

Malvasia del Vulture

Grapes of the Malvasia variety.

Wine suitable for ageing. Bright, pale straw colour; distinct aroma to which is added a subtle scent of almond blossom. Sweet taste, delicate, well-balanced, white natural froth.

Alcohol content very variable, according to the vintage year, from 11 to 16% by vol., total acidity 0.5%.

Sparkling dessert wine. To be served very cold (40 degrees F.).

Main places of production:

Rapolla
Rionero in Vulture
Ripacandida

Moscato del Vulture

Grapes of the Muscat variety.

Pale straw colour, very limpid. Very delicate aroma typical of the grape. Delicately sweet taste, velvety. White natural froth.

Alcohol content very variable, according to the year of vintage, from 10 to 15% by vol, total acidity 0.5%.

Sparkling dessert wine. To be served very cold (40 degrees F.).

Main places of production:

> Barile
> Moschito
> Ripacandida

Aglianico del Vulture

Grapes of the Aglianico variety.

Suitable for ageing. Garnet red colour, bright; pleasant aroma typical of strawberries and violets. Dry, tasty, fresh, somewhat astringent and tannic; with age, becomes austere, velvety, warm, full-bodied, and harmonious. Vivid blood red and very fine froth.

Alcohol by vol. 12-14%, total acidity 0.5%.

Superior table wine which is excellent with "cutturiddu", a lamb stew with small onions. If properly aged, suitable with red and white-meat roasts. Recommended with highly flavoured and hot dishes. To be served at room temperature.

Main places of production:

> Barile
> Rapolla
> Rionero in Vulture

Calabria

Among the most lasting of my childhood memories are the times when the whole of my family went to Fracà for the grape-harvest. My Father had planted a vine-yard and built a large cellar, well-furnished with barrels, which seemed almost like a church. During the pressing of the grapes, I remember the must which coloured brightly the feet and legs of the pressers, impregnated with the red and white fruit which became Castiglione and Greco. These scenes have remained imprinted on my mind all my life.

Once, I recall, without realising it I turned the spigot of a cask which let out a jet of Castiglione. Fortunately I was able to turn it off in time but I could not avoid being reproved by my Mother and by one of our helpers, Mariano. This episode during my youth was the inspiration, many years later, for one of my most important stories "Cacciadiavoli", a drama in which Castiglione plays the leading role.

I do not know whether Castiglione is among the most famous of Calabrian wines, but sure it is that, with its heavy, black-red grape mixed with Greco, Insolia, Malvasia and Nocera, a wine of high alcohol content (15%) is made which is used for enriching other much lighter and less tasty wines.

It is the wine for good, strong palates, which accompanies good food and it is also the wine which reigns over the contest of "Padrone e Sotto" (Master and Under-Master), a game in which knives flash when the Master decides not to offer a glass to the person chosen by the Under-Master. The contest then becomes rough having reached a point of honour because the drinker left high and dry suffers the humiliation imposed upon him for a minute or two, but then he pulls out his knife and strikes. Thus the murderous Castiglione makes the blood also run, much less thick and perfumed than itself.

Even though I have never been a great wine drinker, finding a bottle of Fracà on the table takes me back to the early days of my life when, after a grape-harvest, the whole family hoped to sell the wine at a good price and, when this did not happen, everyone in Palmi and Piana di Gioia was full of anxiety and worry on account of the disappointment.

The period of Castiglione ended for me with the earthquake of December 28th. We moved to Turin where Grignolino, Barbera and Freisa among the red wines of the North tried to replace our native wine.

After some years of exile, I returned to Calabria which to me meant reuniting myself with the old traditions, the smells of local cooking such as swordfish, bean and chick-pea soup and, above all, with Castiglione. But Mariano had acquired the old farm, Pietrosa, where the grapes, from which "Tre Are" was made, were cultivated. This is a rosé wine in which the coast melts all its smells of earth and rocks.

But the labourers had neglected the vine, preferring to live on other food which was easier to grow. Mariano had no time to tend it and he died too young — 37 years of age — before he had time to put it in order again. I was unable to rebuild it and so, with a sad heart, I substituted olive trees for the vines which, to tell the truth, have been very satisfactory.

284

The disappearance of the vine from Pietrosa did not, however, mean the disappearance of "Tre Are" from my table because surrounding my land are many friends and farmers who, each time I return there, hurry to bring me local wine, eggs and fruit in great quantities. And the wine is "Tre Are", a nectar, which is drunk after the dessert course, at the end of a meal, before the coffee. It is a wine which can be compared with the best Italian and foreign brands, always on condtion, however, that the attentive care of the cultivator is also ever present during the wine-making. Unfortunately not all the Calabrians are as meticulous as the Tuscans and Pugliesians in the production of their wine. To this end, an efficient working organisation for wine production in Calabria could, through the application of modern methods, give excellent results.

But one day in the not too distant future we hope that the production of Calabrian wines will be able to enter the national, and indeed the international, market, enlivening the tables with Mottorossa di Calabria, with Cirò, Greco di Gerace, Pèllaro, San Sidero and many others; this would be the most just recognition of the region with the wish that soon it may join the other Italian regions in economic development.

CATANZARO

Cirò

Grapes of the Magliocco (90%) and Greco Bianco (10%) varieties.

Suitable for long ageing. Deep ruby red colour, which changes to orange with age, bright. Intense aroma. Sweetish to the palate, becoming austere with age, generous, alcoholic. When very old it becomes a rich and aristocratic tonic and makes a safe, comforting drink; recommended for the therapy of convalescents.

Alcohol by vol. 15%, total acidity 0.55%.

Excellent table wine and, when well aged, suitable with strong cheeses; a dessert wine. To be served at room temperature.

Main places of production:

Cirò
Melissa

A wine very similar to Cirò is produced in some localities in the so-called Hills of Crotone.

Greco Rosso also called Greco Rosso di Pontegrande

Grapes of the Greco Nero (50%), Nerello (35%) and Greco Bianco (15%) varieties.

Mature after 2 years, perfect at 5. Vivid cherry red colour; intense aroma, dry taste, sincere, generous.

Alcohol by vol. 12-13%, total acidity 0.55%.

Excellent table wine, if properly aged, suitable with red and white meat-roasts. It is best drunk, however, especially when young, with innumerable Calabrian specialties prepared with aubergines, except, of course, those dishes prepared with vinegar. To be served at room temperature.

Main places of production:

Gragliano
Pentone
Pontegrande

San Sidero

Grapes of the Magliocco (50%) and Marsigliana (50%) varieties.

Suitable for ageing. Variable depness of ruby red colour, bright; intense vinous aroma. Tasty, generous, sincere. It becomes a typical brick red with age and acquires a special taste which brings it close to Marsala.

Alcohol by vol. 13-14%, total acidity 0.7%.

Superior table wine; when well aged, very good with

OR.F.E.VI.

VINO NOBILE
DI MONTEPULCIANO

ENOPOLIO DI POGGIBONSI
SIENA ITALY

OR·FE·VI·

Frascati

Produced and Bottled in Italy by

FEDERAZIONE ITALIANA **DEI CONSORZI AGRARI**

Stabilimento Vinicolo di Frascati (Vermicino)

Net Contents 1 Pt. 8 Fl. Oz. - Alc. 12% By Vol.

Y vini vecchi delle grandi annate della Cremosina e di altri cantoni—

Vino vecchio
Nebbiolo
della vendemmia 1802
lasciato diventare amaro

〜∘〜

(Uve dei vigneti di Val Maggiore e degli Ochetti presso la Vezza cedute dai Signori Sola in cambio dei nostri Moscati e Bracchetti. Trasportate dal mezzadro Dionigi e pigiate nella cantina della Cremosina)

〜∘〜

Dalla Cremosina nella Settimana Santa del 1806 — Il Conte Giulio—

Confezione depositata

ETICHETTA ORIGINALE DEL PRIMO OTTOCENTO MESSA A STAMPA DAL

Dr. Arturo Bersano, proprietario Nizza Monferrato (Asti)

NEBBIOLO VECCHIO		VEZZA D'ALBA

vendemmia in Piemonte alla cascina Bersano

Riserva numerata bottiglia

Invecchiato e imbottigliato all'origine

Dr. Arturo Bersano

DEPOSITATA

Vino Cortese Secco

Dr. ARTURO BERSANO · Cascina Cremosina NIZZA MONF. (Asti)

strong cheeses and especially with sheep's milk cheese, from Crotone.

Main places of production:

>Gizzeria
>Sambiase
>Sant'Eufemia Lamèzia

COSENZA

Moscato di Cosenza

Grapes of the Moscato variety.
Suitable for maturing. Colour varies from pale straw to amber. Very delicate aroma. Moderately sweet taste, velvety, warm, pleasant.
Alcohol by vol. 15-16%, which increases with age up to 18%.
Superior dessert wine. Blends very well with "Cassatelle della Sila", a doughnut filled with a mixture of fresh cheese, eggs, sugar and milk and cooked in the oven.
It is produced in small quantities in several districts of the province.
The following wines are rightly famous: Moscato di Frascineto from the vineyards of Frascineto; Moscato di Saracena, produced mostly from the Guarnaccio variety of grapes to which is added a small quantity of Moscatello grapes, to give the typical aroma. Golden yellow colour. It reaches 18% by vol. of alcohol content.

Pollino

Grapes of the Magliocco, Nerello, Verdana, Malvasia Bianca and Montonico varieties.

Immediately ready for consumption, although suitable for ageing.

Variable deepness of ruby red colour; sincere bouquet. Dry taste, delicate, fine, well-balanced.

Alcohol by vol. 13%, total acidity 0.5%.

Excellent table wine; if well matured, suitable with white-meat roasts. It blends very well with roast dormice.

Main places of production:

Castrovillari
Frascineto
San Barile

Savuto

Grapes of the Magliocco (50%), Greco Nero (20%), Pecorello (20%), and Malvasia Bianca (10%) varieties.

Suitable for maturing. Rather deep ruby red colour, which acquires garnet reflections with age. Light characteristic aroma. Dry taste, slightly velvety, warm, generous.

Alcohol by vol. 13%, total acidity 0.6%.

Superior table wine; when well matured, suitable with red and white-meat roasts.

Main places of production:

Marzi
Rogliano

Lacrima di Castrovillari

Grapes of the Lacrima vatriety.

Beautiful garnet red colour which tends to brick red with age. Full aroma, dry and full taste.

It is produced in the district of Castrovillari.

Greco di Gerace

Grapes of the Greco di Gerace variety.

Suitable for moderate ageing. Vivid amber-yellow colour, bright. Typical aroma of the grape to which an aroma of orange blossom is added, creating a fragrant bouquet. Sweet taste, soft, full, perfectly blended, sustained and fine quality.

Alcohol by vol. 16-17%, total acidity 0.7%.

Great dessert wine. To be served very cold.

It is produced in small quantities, in a wide area between the back of the Apennines and the La Verde and Torbido rivers and further up to the municipality of Gioiosa.

Mostly produced from the hills between Gerace and Locri.

Pellaro

Grapes of the Nerello, Nocera and Alicante varieties.

Suitable for moderate ageing. Vivid, pink colour, tending to ruby red, very limpid. Typical vinous aroma, mostly due to the Alicante variety of grapes. Slightly sweet to the palate; sincere, generous, strong.

Alcohol by vol. 16-17, total acidity 0.5-0.6%.

Excellent table wine, when well aged, outstanding with "fricandeau" and "brasati". To be served at room temperature.

Mostly produced between Capo dell'Anni and Punta di Pellaro, near Reggio Calabria.

Sicilia

The wines produced in Sicily are strong, rich in flavour and impetuous, wines which flash like a knife and which leave the unprepared drinker more dead than alive. The lower classes liken it, with an almost poetical association, to Etna - to lava and fire. At Trecastagni, near Catania, in the district of St. Alfio, a feast is held during the month of May to which the faithful from all the neighbouring villages come.

After the various religious ceremonies, this feast becomes the true triumph of the Sicilian horse and carriage: these are dressed all over with plumes, with collars from which hang innumerable small bells, with buckles and with caparisons, to carry the faithful to Trecastagni. The most impressive part of this feast is therefore after the services in church, when the procession of carriages, overloaded with passengers who in their turn are well loaded with wine, re-enters the villages at night to the infernal noise of bells, the cracking of whips and the cries of "Long live Saint Alfio" from the crowds which line the pavements.

We have spoken of strong wines, but in Sicily there are also sweet, aromatic wines with deep and changing reflections which, to a connoisseur, are not even wines inasmuch as they are associated with biscuits and plates full of little cakes.

The geography of the vine in Sicily is continuously moving: the small wine-maker, who produces wine just for the family cellar, tires of turning the earth after the vine has completed its cycle and every twenty years he moves his vineyard to another place and begins another cycle. The Sicilian vine may therefore be described as nomadic, but it is always vigorous and maintains its good quality.

The merits of Sicilian wine can be connected with the history of Sicily at the time of the glorious Expedition of the Thousand. At the famous battle of Calatafimi, Garibaldi, hoping for a gesture of friendship from the Bourbons, had given the order to hold fire; but the hot-headed Sicilian boys took no notice, with an unexpected result.

While waiting at the farm of Baron Mistretta to join Garibaldi's forces, these boys emptied many barrels of wine and, when the Bourbons came into sight, they began to shout insults and shower them with abuse. The Bourbons left their positions and advanced in order to retaliate until they were aware that there was another group of boys, who had simply climbed up on the rocks so that they could see and enjoy the spectacle better, behind them. Thinking that they were surrounded by superior forces, the Bourbons began to go back. At that moment Garibaldi's troops arrived and the retreat of the Bourbons turned into an inglorious flight.

A well-known Italian film director, following the road from Marsala to Palermo while making a documentary film on the itinerary of "The Thousand", found Baron Mistretta's estate completely changed. "But is Baron Mistretta's wine still made in these parts?" the director asked some farm labourers. They knew the whole story of Calatafimi and they told it to him just as their fathers had told it to them. Then they brought him some wine in which green and golden reflections danced. It was the impetuous wine of Garibaldi which is still produced to-day on the hills where "The Thousand" fought — the wine which opened the road to Palermo for the heroes.

CATANIA

Etna Bianco

Grapes of the Trebbiano and Inzolia varieties.
Suitable for ageing. Greenish white colour with golden
reflections; rich bouquet. Dry, tasty, delicate, well-balanced.
Alcohol by vol. 11-12%, total acidity 0.55-0.6%.
Produced in the area around the vulcano Etna, in the pro-
vince of Catania.

Etna Rosato

Grapes of the Catarratto and Trebbiano varieties.
Beautiful pink colour, very limpid, fragrant aroma. Dry,
tasty, soft, fresh, smooth.
Alcohol by vol. 12%, total acidity 0.55%.

Excellent table wine; to be recommended with soups. To be served rather cool.

Produced in the same area as the Etna Bianco.

Etna Rosso

Grapes of the Sangiovese, Morello and Trebbiano varieties. Suitable for ageing. It is bottled after 3 years of being kept in barrels of Slavonic oak. Vivid ruby red colour, bright; full bouquet. Dry, tasty, genuine, noble and sustained quality, well-balanced.

Alcohol by vol. 11.5-12%, total acidity 0.55%.

Excellent table wine and, when well aged, suitable with red and white-meat roasts and game.

To be served at 60 degrees F.

Ragalna Bianco

Greenish white colour, delicate aroma, dry taste with a pleasantly acidulous touch, fresh and slightly sparkling.

Main places of production:

> Adrano
> Paternò
> Santa Maria di Nicosia

Vino bianco di Mila

Whitish colour with greenish reflections, very limpid, of subtle aroma, dry taste, acidulous and fresh with a low alcohol content, produced in small quantities.

MESSINA

Capo Bianco

Grapes of the Catarratto Bianco, Catarratto Lucido, Greca-
nico, Catanese Bianco and Panse Precoce varieties.
Suitable for maturing. Very pale straw colour, bright; delicate
aroma. Dry, tasty, moderately alcoholic, smooth, harmonious.
Alcohol by vol. 12-12.5%, total acidity 0.6-0.7%.
Outstanding wine suitable with fish. It is excellent with
grilled swordfish. To be served at 50 degrees F.
Produced at Milazzo

Malvasia di Lipari

"The much-praised ambrosia of the Gods is made of nothing
but Malvasia, which is produced from a vine planted at
Lipari". Abbot Meli.
Grapes of the Malvasia of Lipari variety.
Suitable for moderate maturing. Golden yellow colour,
bright; intense, suave aroma. Delicately sweet taste, velvety,
full, soft and mellow and of consistent quality; well-balanced,
exquisite.
Alcohol by vol. 14-16%, total acidity 0.5%.
Great dessert wine. To be served at 50 degrees F.
It is produced in the Island of Salina and also in small
quantities in the Island of Stromboli.

Mamertino

Grapes of the Catarratto Bianco, Catarratto Lucido and Inzolia
varieties mostly, together with Grillo and Grenache Bianco
varieties.
Suitable for moderate ageing. Golden yellow colour, intense
aroma.
It is produced in two types: one dry with a distinct, sweetish
touch, and one delicately sweet and velvety.

Average alcohol by vol. 15-17%, total acidity 0.5%.

The first type is a fish wine, outstanding with a local dish, the "sciabacheddu", small, newly-born, fried fishes. The second type is a dessert wine. To be served at 50 degrees F.

It is produced in many places almong the Tyrrhenian coast. Particularly good at:

> Castroreale Bagni
> Rometta
> Santa Lucia del Mela

Taormina

Grapes of the Cararratto Bianco, Carricante, Damaschina, Grillo, Inzolia, and Minnella Bianca varieties.

Suitable for moderate ageing. Pale straw colour, light aroma. Dry taste, genuine, fresh, moderately alcoholic, pleasant.

Alcohol by vol. 11-13%, total acidity 0.6-0.7%.

Wine to be served with fish. To be served at 50 degrees F.

Main places of production:

> Gaggi
> Graniti
> Taormina

Capo Rosso

Grapes of the Nocera, Nerello, Cappuccio, Nerello Mascalese, Nerello d'Avola, Barbera and Sangiovese varieties.

Suitable for moderate ageing. Pink, tending to ruby red colour, light aroma. Dry, tasty, full, harmonious.

Alcohol by vol. 13-13.5%, total acidity 0.6-0.7%.

Good table wine. To be served at 60 degrees F.

Produced along the Tyrrhenian coast of the Province of Messina Divieto and Olivieri.

Faro

"A selected group of wines from Faro Superiore and Alcamo
[improves
the 'grand finale'.
They exude a sense of euphoria and instill their musical warmth
into my epic poetry,
Reason for great joy".

> *Eletta schiera il gran finale allargano*
> *quelli del Faro Superiore e d'Alcamo;*
> *nell'epa mia cantoria un senso stillano*
> *diffuso d'euforia,*
> *e un lor calore musicale infondono,*
> *motivo d'allegoria.*
>
> Augusto Moreli

Grapes of the Nerello Mascalese, Nerello Cappuccio, Nerello
d'Avola, Nocera, Citana Nera and other varieties.
Suitable for ageing; mature after 2 years, perfect at 5.
Vivid ruby red colour, bright; delicate bouquet with a
distinct orange aroma. Dry, sincere, generous, tasty, well-
balanced.
Alcohol by vol. 12.5-13%, total acidity 0.65-0.7%.
Outstanding wine with red and white-meat roasts, fowl and
all game. To be served at 60 degrees F.

Main places of production:

Faro Superiore
Ganzini

PALERMO

Partinico Bianco

Grapes of local varieties.
Pale straw colour with amber reflections, delicate aroma.
It undergoes a preliminary ageing of 3 years in small barrels

of mulberry wood. Dry taste, genuine, full-bodied which greatly improves with age until it aquires, after about 10 years, the warm and round taste of a good Malaga.

Alcohol by vol. 16%, total acidity 0.6-0.7%.

When well matured, it is an exceptional aperitive which must be served very cold (42 degrees F.). When young, outstanding with fish soups. To be served at 50 degrees F.

Main places of production:

Monreale

Partinico

RAGUSA

Cerasuolo di Vittoria

Grapes of the Frappata (mostly), Calabrese, Grossonero and Albanello varieties.

Suitable for very long ageing (30 years). Beautiful cherry colour which becomes ashen white with age, bright; full bouquet in which the aroma of jasmine and pomegranate may be detected. Dry taste with a pleasant slightly bitter touch, neutral, full-bodied, warm.

Alcohol by vol. 16%, total acidity 0.6-0.7%.

Excellent table wine. To be served at 60 degrees F.; when very old it is an outstanding aperitif. To be served cold (40 degrees F.).

Main places of production:

Acate

Ragusa

Vittoria

ORFEVI

Arneo

ROSATO
"ROSÉ WINE,,

FEDEXPORT
ITALIA

Produced and bottled in Italy by

STABILIMENTO DI RUBIERA

FEDERAZIONE ITALIANA DEI CONSORZI AGRARI

NET. CONT. 24 FL. OZ. · ALC. 13% BY VOL.

OR.FE.VI.
TORTORICI

MARSALA
SUPERIOR DRY

PRODUCED AND BOTTLED IN SICILY - ITALY BY

STABILIMENTO MAZARA DEL VALLO (MARSALA)
FEDERAZIONE ITALIANA CONSORZI AGRARI

NET CONT. 1 PT. 6 FL. OZ. - ALC. 18% BY VOL.

Rivera

ROSSO
STRAVECCHIO
RISERVA

P.&S. de Corato
AZIENDA VINICOLA DELLE TENUTE RIVERA
ANDRIA (Bari) ITALY

CONTENTS 1 PT. 8 FL. OZ.
ALCOHOL 11,5 % BY VOL.

Rivera

BIANCO
Castel del Monte
Dry White Wine

PRODUCED AND BOTTLED BY
P. & S. de Corato
AZIENDA VINICOLA DELLE TENUTE RIVERA
ANDRIA (Bari) ITALY

SIRACUSA

Albanello di Siracusa

Grapes of the Albanello variety.
It is matured for 8-10 years in oak barrels. Beautiful golden yellow colour, subtle penetrating aroma. Dry taste, with a distinct bitter touch, very pleasing, warm, full, generous, well-balanced.
Alcohol by vol. 17-18%, total acidity 0.75%.
A great aperitif. To be served well chilled (50 degrees F.).
A sweet type is also produced but is not to be recommended.

Main places of production:

> Floridia
> Siracusa

Eloro Bianco

Grapes of the Albanello, Catarratto Bianco and Grillo varieties.
Suitable for maturing. Deep straw colour; distinct "sui generis" aroma. Dry taste, light typical taste of scorched wine, fresh, harmonious.
Alcohol by vol. 13-15%, total acidity 0.5%.
Good table wine suitable with fish. To be served at 50 degrees F.

Main places of production:

> Avola
> Noto

Moscato di Noto

Grapes of the Muscat variety.
Beautiful, bright golden yellow colour. Fragrant bouquet.
Moderately sweet taste, sincere, smooth, exquisite.

Alcohol by vol. 14-16%, total acidity 0.5%.

Great wine to be served between meals. To be served at 57 degrees F.

Main places of production:

Noto
Pachino

Pollio - Moscato di Siracusa

"Oh my sweet Muscat! born in the hills of Syracuse".

Ianus Anysius.

Grapes of the yellow Muscat variety.

Beautiful, bright, golden yellow colour. Typical intense aroma of grapes. Fairly sweet taste, full, generous, harmonious, exquisite.

Alcohol by vol. 16%, total acidity 0.5%.

Great wine to be served between meals. To be served at 60 degrees F.

It is the most ancient Muscat wine history refers to. It seems to have been produced for the first time by King Pollius who, in the 7th. century B.C., brought the vines to Syracuse from Biblina, a part of Thrace, where they originated.

Main place of production:

Siracusa

Eloro Rosso

Grapes of the Calabrese variety.

Suitable for ageing. Deep garnet red colour, light aroma.

Dry taste, sincere, full, strong, well-balanced.

Alcohol by vol. 13-16%, total acidity 0.5-0.6%.

Good table wine and, if well matured, suitable with roasts. To be served at 60 degrees F.

Main places of production:

Avola

Noto

TRAPANI

Marsala

Marsala comes from the Arabic "Marsh-El-Allah", which means Harbour of God, and this is a name full of meaning for whoever loves wine.

Marsala wine is warm and generous, with a charateristic aroma, of golden yellow colour; it is a typical dessert wine, in great demand and much appreciated for its invigorating action.

It is produced in the area typical to this wine, limited by the law passed on 4th. November 1950, no. 1069, and which includes towns in three provinces: in the province of Trapani, (Campobello, Castelvetrano, Marsala, Mazara del Vallo, Trani); in the province of Palermo (Balestrate, Partinico, San Cipirello, San Giuseppe Iato, Terrasini Favorotta, Trappeto) and in the province of Agrigento (Menfi, Sciacca).

Marsala wine must be put on sale with the following denominations:

a) Marsala fine (Italia, I.P., Particolare) with an alcohol content of not less than 17% by volume;

b) Marsala superiore (S.O.M., Garibaldi Dolce, G.D., L.P.) with an alcohol content of not less than 18% by volume;

c) Marsala vergine (Soleras) with an alcohol content of not less than 18% by volume;

d) Marsala speciale (Marsala all'Uovo, Crema Marsala, Marsala alla Mandorla, alla Fragola, al Caffè, etc., etc.) with an alcohol content of not less than 18% by volume.

The law of 4th. November 1950 was completed by a

Regulation which, while prescribing the standard of production and the characteristics of Marsala wine, imposes periods of ageing under governmental control.

Marsala wine is considered one of the most famous Italian classical wines on account of its origin and particular qualities. As a matter of fact, it is interesting to know this aristocratic wine's history which is connected which the period of the Napoleonic wars:

During the second half of the 18th. century, two Englishmen, young merchants from Liverpool, John and William Woodhouse, full of talent and initiative, went to Sicily, to Marsala, in order to buy raw material for the manufacture of soda and their attention was drawn to the high alcohol content of the local wine and by its similarity to the famous wines of Portugal and of Spain.

Immediately realising the possibility of creating a type of wine like Madeira, which is very well-known and appreciated in England, the Woodhouses, who certainly must have known the method of processing the famous Spanish, Portuguese and Canary Island wines, considered that Marsala, like Cadice and Madeira, being more or less in the same latitude, was crossed by the same isothermal lines, that is that it had the same average annual temperature.

Profiting from these circumstances and their attention being drawn to the magnificent characteristics of these wines which came from sunny vineyards and which, when properly matured and treated, were just as good as those from Spain and Portugal, they set up in Marsala, in 1773, a large industry for the making and exportation of the local wine which they called "Marsala Wine".

In the beginning, the general orientation of production was towards the making of high quality wines, destined to be exported overseas and Lord Nelson said, "Marsala wines are so good that any gentleman may allow them on his table". Then, little by little, the possibility of distribution in the Kingdom of Naples and in other places showed the advantage of producing other types of wine, which, while maintaining the fundamental characteristics of the Marsala type, possessed them to a lesser degree, so that they would be accessible, as regards price, to the poorer people too.

The beginning of the parallel development of the various qualities, which characterises so distinctly the history of this famous wine, is the undertaking by the Woodhouses to supply the English fleet in the Mediterranean, then under the command of the First Lord of the Admiralty, Horatio Nelson, Duke of Bronte, with Marsala wine.

The oldest historical event related to Marsala wine was, in fact, the sailing from the Port of Trapani in 1773 of H.M.S. "Elizabeth" to England with a cargo of sixty barrels of Marsala Wine.

The oldest document regarding the existence of the lesser Marsala wines is, however, a contract in which the above-mentioned First Lord of the Admiralty, on 19th. March 1800, bought 500 casks of Marsala Wine from John and William Woodhouse, to be delivered free of shipping and every other charge and "without loss of time" to Her Majesty's ships in Malta. The contract is signed by Lord Nelson and by John Woodhouse. Even to-day, this document is jealously kept by the Woodhouse family.

In 1800, Napoleon was fighting against England also on the seas. The two fleets met first at Aboukir and then at Trafalgar; in these two memorable battles, the Franco-Spanish fleet was defeated. The memory of Nelson, who died gloriously in the Battle of Trafalgar, and his great victories, contributed largely to the spreading of knowledge amongst the English of that wine with which their victorious fleet had been supplied.

At first the production of Marsala Wine was limited to high-quality types; it was only at the beginning of this century that the industry created new types of Marsala called "Special Marsala" among which is the excellent Egg Marsala which, on account of its therapeutic qualities, has had a great success.

Marsala Wine production reaches five hundred thousand hundredweight per year.

Alcamo

Grapes of the Catarratto, Inzolia, Grillo and other local varieties.

Whitish straw colour, almost pure white, light aroma. Dry, tasty, sincere, generous and fresh.

Alcohol by vol 13-15%, total acidity 0.6%.

Excellent table wine, suitable with fish. To be served at 50 degrees F.

Moscato di Pantelleria

Grapes of the Zibibbo variety.

Amber yellow colour, very limpid. Penetrating aroma characteristic of grapes. Sweet taste, full bodied, velvety, fragrant and generous.

Alcohol by vol. 15%, total acidity 0.65%.

Great dessert wine and recommended with fruit. To be served at 50 degrees F.

Produced in the Isle of Pantelleria.

Sardegna

The true drinker is moderate in his drink as the virile man is moderate in love.   I like Azorin's theory, according to which Don Giovanni Tenorio was not a real man!   This moderation is necessary above all for those who have to drink any Sardinian wine whatsoever.   Contrary to what is generally believed, Sardinians are not taciturn; they are sparing of words, not usually extravagant with them, but they are extraordinarily discreet, even circumspect and mistrustful, both of their own words and of those of others.

Every Sardinian tries to overcome this atavistic mistrust of words with a glass of wine.   He drinks with friends and the wine helps to nourish liking and friendship.   Whoever has been our guest in Sassari, Nuoro Oristano or Quarto, or even Alghero or Sorso, knows how important it is for the Sardinian to drink in company, and how hard is this experience.   Naturally I am referring to the high qualities of the wines, such as Girò, Moscato of Campidano, Malvasia of Bosa, Vermentino, Nasco, Monica, Oliena, Torbato of Alghero, the metaphysical Moscato of Luras, the noble Canonau of Sorso and, above all, Vernaccia. All names which carry special meanings for just a few people because only recently have the Sardinian wines become known outside the island.

The connoisseur has no need of my guidance. For the inexperienced and the apprentice to wine I could say, for example, that Girò has characteristics which remind one of Port, Nasco has some which remind one of Hungarian Tokaj and Spanish Sherry, and Monica has some which remind one of Malaga. Of course, they are approximate comparisons which, at the most, may help as a first bearing or introduction.

Everyone drinks and tastes wine in his own way and, in his own way, remembers it. I can think only of the mountains whose compact, wooded slopes lie high above the small village of Oliena, hidden in the bottom of the valley which is dominated by the hill of Ortobene and where the procession, described by Grazia Deledda in "Elias Portolu", of men on horseback with the women riding pillion winds every year for the Feast of the Redeemer. On the other hand, poets have sung the praises of wine since the world began, even if they have done so only vaguely and approximately. They praise wine in general and they make a metaphysical entity out of the joy of wine. But sometimes a particular wine catches their fancy, like a face or a voice. Gabriele d'Annunzio, in his preface to Hans Barth's "Osteria", describes the wine of Oliena, famous in Sardinia, as a nectar with the colour of fire, with a perfume of a rose garden.

For centuries, the genuine Vernaccia has been Sardinian and has meant Sardinia. It is so Sardinian and so different from all other wines, both from the island and from abroad, either homonymous or not, that it makes one think that it is really autochthonous, as in the legend of Saint Giustina, patron saint of Oristano, who one day was passing over the plain, which was parched by drought, and who was touched by the sight of the desolation spread there by malaria and the bad Spanish rule. The story is that the slender vine with the slender leaves was born from the very pure tears which flowed from her imploring eyes raised towards the sky.

I am inclined to believe that the miraculous little plant consoled our forefathers also in more ancient times, because on the plain of Oristano, near Solarussa and Milis, just where the vines are cultivated and the most valued wines are made, the vineyards are still looked after by the same methods that Columella taught the Latin farmers. Straight rows, well stretched out on the plain; the branch of the vine springs from the trunk which is pruned down to earth level and a cane stake supports it a metre from the ground. The bunches of grapes are delicate and turgid like nipples; it is sufficient to pile them up together for the must to run out from every part, so thin is the skin of the fruit. The wine which comes from these delicate bunches is, however, very strong; once it has fermented, it keeps for years without spoiling: in its first year of life, Vernaccia is weak, pale, without joy, without aroma and almost tasteless; it clears and starts to become interesting under the heat of the following Summer's sun; in Autumn, that is at the beginning of its second year, it is very pleasant to drink but has not yet developed the qualities which are resplendent during the second Summer: then Vernaccia is perfect, it has acquired its bright amber colour and its tonic qualities, slightly exciting and highly strengthening.

In order to go to Sardinia, it is enough to reserve in time a place on the boat which sails from Civitavecchia or from Leghorn; but once there, you must look for friends and wine. If you know how to look, you will find friends who are true and wine which is genuine.

CAGLIARI

Vernaccia

Grapes of Vernaccia.
Mature after 4 years, perfect et 10-15 years. Golden yellow colour exquisite tipical flavour. Dry sligthly sweetish tart, harmonious.
Alcohol by vol. 15-18%, total acidity 0.55%.
Great wine for hors d'oevres, particularly appreciated whit fitsh. To be served at 45 degrees F.

Main places of production:

>Baratili San Pietro
>Cabras
>Oristano
>Santa Giusta
>Simaxis

Monica

Grapes of Monica.

Matured after 3 years, perfect at 6-8 vivid ruby red colour; lasting delicate aroma wich tending to become orange with a subtle bitter after-taste, very pleasing, velvety, warm, harmonious.

Alcohol by vol. 15-18%, total acidity 0.35-0.55%.

Exceptional with fruit or as an after-dinner wine, to be served at 45 degrees F.

Main place of production:

Campidano di Cagliari

Nasco

Grapes of nasco.

Suitable for ageing. Beautiful golden yellow colour, subtle penetrating aroma of nasco. Dry taste. with a distinct bitter touch, very pleasing, warm full, generous, wele balanced.

Alcohol vol. 15-18%, total acidity 0.75%.

Great dessert wine, and with fruit. To be served at 55 degrees F.

Main places of production:

Campidano di Cagliari
Oristano

NUORO

Malvasia di Bosa

Grapes of the Malvasia variety.

Beautiful golden yellow colour with greenish reflections, shiny; more intense aroma than that of Malvasia del Campidano di

Cagliari. Dry taste, velvety, sincere, generous, harmonious.
Alcohol by vol. 14-17%, total acidity 0.35-0.4%.
Great wine to be served with fish. To be served at 45
degrees F.
Produced in the area of Bosa.

Oliena

"Do you not know the Nepenthes of Oliena, even by name?
How slack! I am sure that, if you had a sip of it, you
would never leave the shade of the snowy rocks and you
would choose for your hermitage one of those small cells
hewn in the stone which the Sardinians call 'Domos de
Janas' (the houses of Janas), and live there like a sponge
in ecstasy amidst small casks and barrels. I know only its
aroma which is beyond description and which was enough to
fill me with rapture". (Gabriele d'Annunzio).
Grapes of the Canonau and Monica varieties.
Suitable for maturing. Ruby red colour sometimes becoming
garnet red and tending toward orange with age; pronounced
aroma of strawberries. Dry, with a characteristic slightly
bitter after-taste of tar, tasty, warm.
The alcohol content is very variable according to the year:
from 12-16% and even higher with maturation.
Excellent table wine; when well matured, to be served with
white and also red-meat roasts. To be served at room
temperature.
Produced from the hills of Oliena.

SASSARI

Torbato Passito

Grapes of the Torbato variety. (The grapes are carefully
taken off the stems and dried for a week in the sun; its
fermentation is topped by the process of alcoholisation).

Beautiful pale straw colour, intense and bright; "sui generis", ethereal bouquet, typical of grapes. Delicately sweet and velvety taste.
Alcohol by vol. 18-19%.
Great dessert wine. To be served at 40 degrees F.

Main places of production:

> Nuraghe Majore
> Pianos de Sozzu

Torbato Secco

Grapes of the Torbato variety.
Beautiful pale straw colour, bright; "sui generis" bouquet, typical of grapes. Dry taste, aromatic, full, harmonious.
Alcohol by vol. 13-14%.
Great wine to be served either with savoury fish dishes (excellent with lobsters "alla Catalana") or as an aperitif. With fish, to be served at 47 degrees F., as an aperitif at 40 degrees F.
Produced in the same places as Torbato Passito.

Vermentino di Gallura

Grapes of the Vermentino variety.
Suitable for maturing. Pale straw colour with amber reflections, bright; typical aroma. Dry, with a pleasant slightly bitter after-taste, delicate, well-balanced.
Alcohol by vol. 14-16, total acidity 0.6%.
Excellent, suitable with fish. To be served at 50 degrees F.
Produced at Santa Teresa Gallura.
A good Muscat wine, "Moscato di Tempio", so-called on account of the district of origin, is produced all over Gallura. It is of pale straw colour and has an intense bouquet; it is delicately sweet, light and frothy.
Alcohol by vol. 13%.

PELLEGRINO

OVOMAL

MARSALA ALL'UOVO

CARLO PELLEGRINO & C.
MARSALA (Prov. di Trapani)

ALCOOL 18 º/o · ZUCCHERI 25 º/o

Scuola del Caravaggio: Fiori e frutta

Anghelu Ruju

Grapes of the Canonau variety. (The grapes are carefully taken off their stems and dried in the sun for a week).

Ruby-cardinal-red colour, pronounced bouquet of cinnamon and the outer husks of nuts. It competes in richness, fullness, quality and harmony with a good Port wine.
Alcohol by vol. 19%.

Great dessert wine. To be served at 64 degrees F.

Produced from the vineyards around the prehistoric town of Anghelu Ruju.

Alphabetical index of the wines

Printed in Italy
by Visigalli-Pasetti arti grafiche
Roma - Viale di Villa Pamphili, 37/1